REMEMBERING Ellicott CITY

REMEMBERING Ellicott CITY

STORIES FROM THE PATAPSCO RIVER VALLEY

JANET KUSTERER
& VICTORIA GOELLER

THE History PRESS

Published by The History Press
Charleston, SC 29403
www.historypress.net

Cover image: *Ellicott City "225"* by Georganne Johnson.

First published 2009

Manufactured in the United States

ISBN 978.1.59629.571.1

Library of Congress Cataloging-in-Publication Data

Kusterer, Janet P.
Remembering Ellicott city : stories from the Patapsco River Valley / Janet Kusterer and Victoria Goeller.
p. cm.
Includes bibliographical references.
ISBN 978-1-59629-571-1
1. Ellicott City (Md.)--History--Anecdotes. I. Goeller, Victoria. II. Title.
F189.E4K873 2009
975.2'81--dc22
2008052955

Notice: The information in this book is true and complete to the best of our knowledge. It is offered without guarantee on the part of the author or The History Press. The author and The History Press disclaim all liability in connection with the use of this book.

From Victoria Goeller: As always, for George and Joe.

From Janet Kusterer: For Tom.

From both of us: Close to the completion of this manuscript we learned of the death of Jean Hannon on October 27, 2008. Both of us are inspired by her determination to get things done, her wonderful sense of humor and her deep love for Ellicott City. She truly made a great difference in our town and she will be sorely missed.

Contents

Acknowledgements

To know Ellicott City is to love it, and we do—especially the rich histories shared with us by so many wonderful people. We appreciate the suggestions and contributions of our husbands, Tom and George, and the input of both of Janet's sons, Rob and Dave. Our lives and our friendship have been enhanced by our partnership and the support of our friends. This project has been a true community endeavor. We gratefully acknowledge the contributions of the citizens of Ellicott City, past and present, the true keepers of its history. Special thanks for the support of Historic Ellicott City, Inc., the Ellicott City Restoration Foundation, Jean Hannon, Herbert Johl, Charlotte Holland, W. Edward Lilley, Tom Sheehan and all those who love Ellicott City and shared their memories and photographs. We look forward to continuing to collect memories of the town to share in the future. If you would like to share your story, call Historic Ellicott City, Inc. at 410-461-6908.

Introduction

In 1975, local community activist Jean Hannon nominated Ellicott City for the National Register of Historic Places. In the nomination she described the town as it has endured for over 235 years:

> *Ellicott City might best be described as a miniature model of an early eighteenth century mill town. Built on seven hills surrounding the Patapsco River valley, the town perches on the granite outcroppings surrounding the area. Streets wind their way down toward Main Street and hence toward the river—a resource that gave the town life and on more than one occasion all but destroyed it.*
>
> *Over 200 18th century buildings—each individually contoured to the steep terrain—offer stark contrast to the sameness of developments in the surrounding county. A busy Main Street bustles a few feet away from a gurgling stream winding past a log cabin on Merryman Street. The Courthouse looks past a row of tiny office buildings known as "Lawyers Row" and across Main Street to the Quaker Meeting House on an opposite hill. The view is unchanged since 1850. In 1975 that's quite distinctive…*
>
> *The Ellicotts, the Carrolls and their descendants perhaps had more influence than any other two families in the area. Henry Clay once made a speech from the front of the Patapsco Hotel and H.L. Mencken spent his summers there as a boy in a house on Church Road. He writes in his book "Happy Days" of first smelling printers ink at the "Times" building… Robert E. Lee was a frequent visitor at Linwood.*

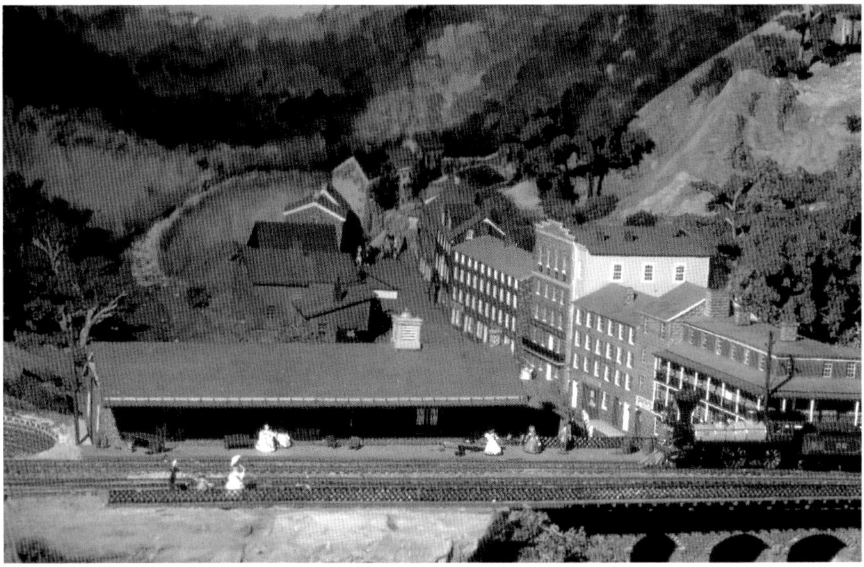

A diorama of Main Street, located in the B&O Railroad Museum, Ellicott City Station. *Courtesy of Historic Ellicott City, Inc.*

Much has changed in the decades since, but many people remember the way it was. Here are some of their stories.

Chapter 1

The Pivotal Year of 1972

The year 1972 was an extraordinary, pivotal time for the town of Ellicott City, Maryland. It was the year of its Bicentennial—two hundred years before, the three Ellicott brothers made their now historic trek from Bucks County, Pennsylvania, here to "The Hollow" to build their mills, their roads and a new way of life for themselves and those around them. While the town was making ambitious plans for an October celebration of that milestone anniversary, disaster struck. In June, one of the worst storms ever to inflict itself on Ellicott City arrived; amazingly, out of the wreckage came rebirth, renewal and a town much stronger than it ever had been.

Tropical Storm Agnes: Remembered by Ned Rogers, John Beck, Ed Lilley and James Robey

Tropical Storm Agnes is one of the most noteworthy events in modern Ellicott City history. It devastated the town and left its future in question. The "hundred year storm" of the twentieth century arrived four years late but just in time for the Bicentennial celebration of Ellicott City. Like the Great Flood of 1868, Tropical Storm Agnes brought death and destruction to the city on the banks of the Patapsco River. The storm caused over $77 million worth of damage to the state of Maryland—the largest ever recorded from a natural disaster in the state's history. Howard County suffered $20 million

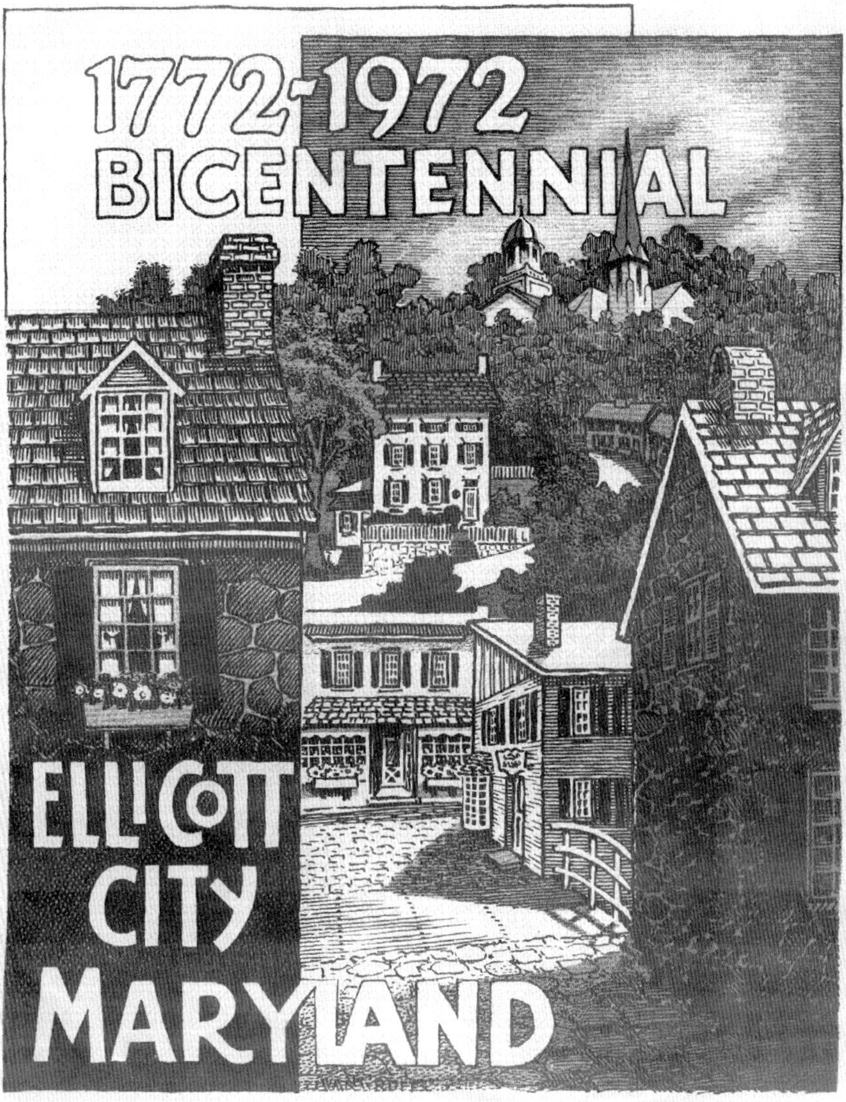

A poster celebrating the Bicentennial of Ellicott City. *Courtesy of Historic Ellicott City, Inc.*

in damages. President Nixon declared most of the state a disaster area and Vice President Agnew visited Ellicott City to assess the damage.

Agnes arrived on the first day of summer, Wednesday, June 21, 1972. Lacking the winds that would have made it a hurricane, Agnes began as a typical summer storm, and people ignored the forecasts of flood watches.

By sunset the downpour increased, overwhelming local streams and creeks that were already swollen from spring storms. At first, there seemed little cause for concern, but by 11:00 p.m. the Patapsco breeched its banks in Ellicott City. Within an hour the water had risen ten feet, flooding lower Main Street.

Ned Rogers was living in an apartment on lower Main Street at the time:

> *A group of us lived in the large stone building in the first block of Main Street in the apartment that is window level with the railroad tracks. There was plenty of construction work around at the time and we had a small store that sold used flannel shirts, candles and denim skirts made from old blue jeans below our apartment. On Saturday nights we would hang out the windows to get some air and watch locals drag race up and down the bottom of Main Street. One weekend it had been raining particularly heavily. A fellow stalled his car under the railroad bridge after passing through the large puddle of standing water numerous times. We sat on the stoop watching him try to get it started for a while, until it finally started to move. Only he wasn't in it.*
>
> *Suddenly we realized the river had risen up to the point it was floating the car away! By the time we started to get things out of the store plenty of things were headed down the river, our "salad" days with them. That was Hurricane Agnes, the end of some old ways of life in Ellicott City and the beginning of a bright new one.*

Throughout the terrible night police, firemen and volunteers alerted people to the danger of the swollen Patapsco. Evacuees were sheltered at the Ellicott City Armory on Montgomery Road, where the 121st Engineer Battalion of the National Guard had been mobilized. On Main Street, residents and merchants rushed to move valuables to the upper stories of buildings. As the water rose to the Odd Fellows Hall on the north side of Main Street and Leidig's Bakery on the south side, midway up Main Street, boat rescues became necessary. Rescuers retrieved members of the Valmas family from the second story of their restaurant at the corner of Main Street and Maryland Avenue. During the night the area lost power and phone service; all those remaining in Main Street buildings were completely cut off from the outside world.

John Beck was asleep in his Tongue Row apartment, just off Main Street, the night that the storm hit the area, just six months after he moved in. He said, "I woke up to the sound of rain, and an emergency vehicle driving down the street, blue light flashing, and a voice on a loudspeaker urging residents to evacuate to high ground. Of course instead of leaving I got up and went to Main Street to see what was going on. The river was rising—the water was lapping at the front of Leidig's Bakery."

As Thursday morning dawned, the extensive damage to Main Street became evident. The river had crested during the night—the town was filled with debris and rubble. The water completely submerged the bridge spanning the Patapsco River and tore the Jonathan Ellicott home in half. Much of Main Street remained under water; more than fifty businesses had been damaged. Nine people died, including eight who died in the Patapsco River in Ellicott City. The ninth died in Columbia. Nine hundred people were left homeless.

Ed Lilley, former owner of the Christmas Company and now Visitor Information Center manager for the Howard County Tourism Council, said:

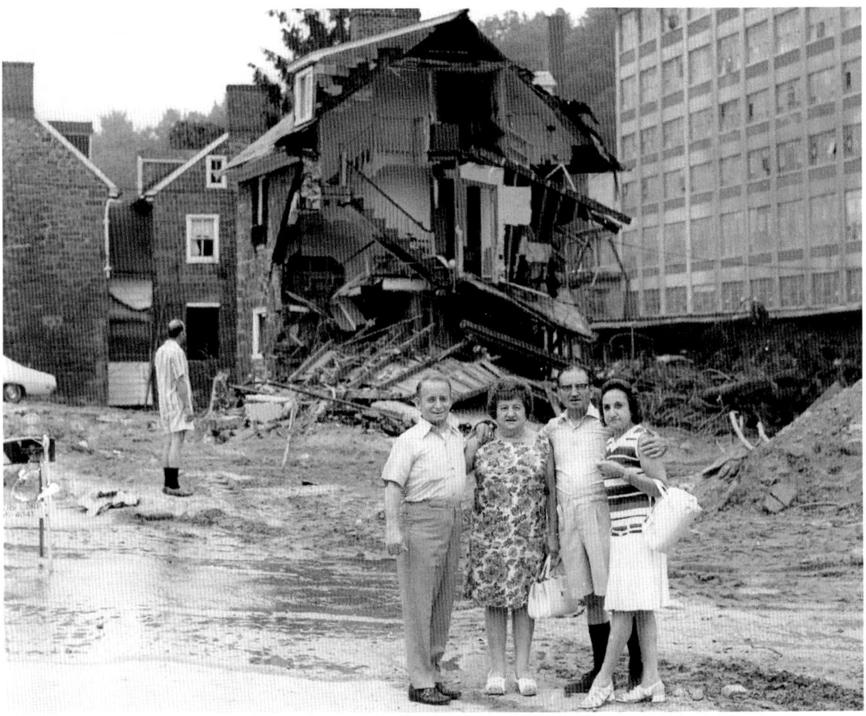

The Jonathan Ellicott House after Tropical Storm Agnes. *Courtesy of DeeDee Lancelotta.*

In 1972, I was working with my father in our insurance business, located on Main Street. When Tropical Storm Agnes hit, I was living nearby at the Town and Country apartments. I was watching a murder mystery on television when the lights went out. The next morning I tried to get to Main Street but was stopped by the police. I showed them my business card and was allowed to proceed. We had many sad phone calls from people asking if their insurance covered them for floods. It was hard to tell most people that they didn't have coverage. I remember one situation where workers were tiling the floor of Healey's Tavern by the river. They kept pushing the tile down, and the tile kept pushing back up—the water from the storm was rising. Ultimately that whole building was lost.

After assessing the damage, people readied themselves for cleanup and renewal. Howard Countians provided homes for flood victims. Local grocery stores stayed open through the night and donated food. The Ellicott City Lions Club acted as a clearinghouse for donated food and clothing.

Once the basic needs of the people had been met, the cleanup began. Volunteers with shovels and buckets joined with community organizations and government agencies. The Army Corps of Engineers cleaned debris from the river, restored bridges and oversaw repair work.

At the time, Jim Robey was a police officer walking the Main Street beat. "Tropical Storm Agnes changed a lot of things," he said. "I was working then, when we got a call about a hand sticking up out of some debris down by the river. I had to walk along the railroad tracks to get to it. It turned out to be a lady I knew from the mill in Daniels, who drowned in the flood. It's hard enough to find any person like that, even harder when you know them."

MUD AND DEBRIS

As a result of Tropical Storm Agnes, the county government updated flood prevention and evacuation plans. Experts identified designated flood areas and initiated construction projects to reduce local flooding. Flow changes along the river are now monitored at strategic points. Although rebuilding continued for some time after, proud residents and merchants were able to celebrate the 200th birthday of Ellicott City in October 1972.

After the storm, Main Street was filled with mud and debris; many buildings had been flooded and were in a state of disrepair. The county considered demolishing downtown Ellicott City, but a dedicated group of citizens decided that it was worth saving. Showcased during the Bicentennial celebration, Ellicott City was enjoying a rekindled interest in the town and its history. Since the services offered by Main Street merchants were being replaced by suburban shopping centers and malls, people wondered if Main Street was still viable.

As property owners began to repair, restore and replace damaged buildings, it became clear that efforts should be made to preserve the exterior design of the buildings. With the support of the Ellicott City Business Association, the county council approved the creation of the Advisory Historic District Commission. Established in October 1972, the mission of the commission was to study and make recommendations to the council for a method by which the historic and architectural heritage of the county could be maintained. Concern about the appropriate historic restoration of the town led the commission to propose "Historic District Zoning" and to appoint a permanent Historic District Commission to review plans for all exterior work performed on buildings in the specific area designated as a historic district. Historic district members of the Bicentennial Celebration Committee and Historic Ellicott Mills assisted the commission, conducting research into the historic and architectural background of the buildings in the district.

In 1973, a committee chaired by Jean Hannon conducted the survey of the proposed historic district. Assisted by Sam Caplan and Dr. Benjamin Mellor, the members conducted exterior surveys, contacted owners, consulted the Hopkins Atlas, researched historic references and dated all the buildings to be included in the historic district.

On February 27, 1974, the Howard County Zoning Board heard testimony to determine the appropriate boundaries for the historic district. The area submitted by the Historic District Commission followed closely the boundaries of the formerly incorporated Ellicott City. There was a sharp divide between supporters and opponents of the creation of a historic district. Many citizens applauded the move to retain the historical significance and integrity of the old mill town. They believed regulating repairs and new construction would ensure a future for Ellicott City. Those in opposition resented the interference of government and feared the regulations would be expensive and cause the loss of control of privately owned property. Opposing members avoided one another for years.

The zoning board approved the creation of the historic district of Ellicott City as proposed by the Historic District Commission on April 24, 1974. It was described as a firm, legally binding mechanism by which all structures

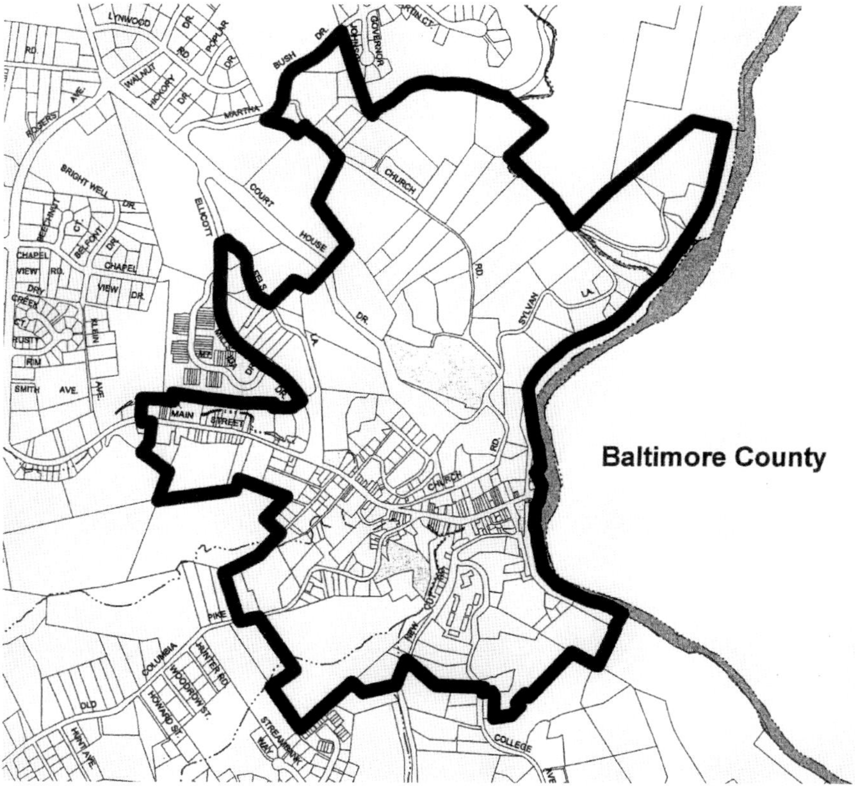

A map of the historic district. © *Howard County government. Used by permission.*

within the Ellicott City Historic District, prior to any construction, moving, demolition, repair or alteration affecting the exterior appearance of such structure, must receive a certificate of approval from the Historic District Commission.

The Historic District Commission continues today. It safeguards the architectural and landscape heritage of Ellicott City as well as Lawyers Hill in Elkridge, a historic district created in 1994. Appointed by the county executive and confirmed by the county council, the commission is composed of seven members, with each historic district represented by one resident or property owner.

Herb Johl spent ten years serving on the Historic District Commission. "One controversial thing we approved of was neon lighting on the outside of the building that once housed the *Times*," he said. "People objected but the building wasn't considered historic. We followed all the rules. Another project that people were concerned about was the proposed senior housing across the Tiber River." (That project was canceled and now Historic Ellicott City, Inc. plans to build a Mill Education Center on the site.)

Celebrations: Interviews with Enalee Bounds, Clare Hoey and Ed Lilley

Enalee Bounds was on the Bicentennial Committee and compiled the commemorative *Bicentennial Journal*, an impressive record of two hundred years of local history. The purpose of the *Journal* was to "review the history of the founding fathers of Ellicott City…and present some items of interest concerning Howard County."

"We asked for everyone's help," Bounds said.

> *We went to museums and historical societies and got copies of information, always making sure we gave credit to our source. We went to the local "big shots" and got them to write stories about the area. I remember going to the Pratt library and reading the old film—it was white printing on a gray background, which made it very hard to read. I'd get too tired to concentrate. The* Howard County Times *staff pasted up the paper for us, and it was on their presses on Main Street when Agnes hit.*
>
> *There was a lot of excitement about the Bicentennial celebration, so I was able to sell a lot of ads for the* Journal. *In fact, I sold so many (and collected all the money due) that I was offered a job selling ads for the* Times. *I turned it down, saying that it was my enthusiasm for the project that made the ad sales such a success.*
>
> *We asked everyone we knew who could write to write stories for us. We covered the earliest history with the Ellicotts and talked about all of the historic sites and events in the area. The celebration lasted a week. The men all grew moustaches and sideburns for the event and wore top hats. Many people wore period dress. The culmination was a huge ball on Saturday at Turf Valley* [Resort and Conference Center], *featuring the Meyer Davis Orchestra, with 865 people attending.*

Herb Johl said, "The railroad station was decorated with images of people painted on the walls and included mice painted in the corners—for a dance held there."

The celebration week ran from October 7 to 14, 1972. Each day had a theme, from "Railroading and Transportation" to "Agriculture and Antiques" to "Ladies' Day." Events included parades—featuring characters from the Enchanted Forest (a children's theme park that opened in suburban Ellicott City in 1955, the same summer that Disneyland opened)—antique shows, a carnival, lunches and walking tours. "This kind of event could only happen in a very small area like ours, and we needed everyone's help," Bounds said. "Then, we didn't want to lose the momentum the event had created. Soon after, a group of us sat on the porch at Lilburn [a landmark in the Historic District] and decided we couldn't let it go. So, Historic Ellicott Mills and the Bicentennial Committee merged, and that was the start of Historic Ellicott City, Inc."

Clare Hoey remembered a photo opportunity from the Bicentennial event:

> *A* Baltimore Sun *Howard County reporter said he would write about us but we had to come up with a picture of some sort to help with the story. This was a great opportunity for us because we had gotten the B&O to go along with the gift "shoppe" idea. So, Ginger Clark took us all over to her mother-in-law's house one morning and we went out to her former smoke house where she had stored trunk loads of old clothing. We spent the morning trying to get ourselves fitted into all those layers of old clothes, and finally we're all assembled on the platform of the station for our picture to be taken. We had to stifle our giggles because we all smelled like smoked ham.*

Twenty-five years later, the town celebrated its 225th anniversary with a yearlong garden party—the EC225 Celebration Gardens Project. Ed Lilley, president of the Ellicott City Restoration Foundation, said, "Cindy Hershberg had the idea to create a garden competition in the historic district in honor of the 225th anniversary of the town in 1997. New gardens were created near the old firehouse, the Main Street rock, Tiber Park and other venues." One of the nicest is at the west end of Main Street, near Ellicott Mills Drive. Created and maintained by the Longfellow Garden Club and called Millstone Park, it features millstones retrieved from the Patapsco River after Tropical Storm Agnes. Another aspect of the celebration was a yearlong salute to Ellicott City fashion called "Our Town—Our Times—Our Clothing." A group of volunteers modeled over two hundred years of styles at a variety of locations around town, including Mount Ida and the Railroad Station Museum. As another part of the 225th celebration, Historic Ellicott City, Inc. installed, carved and painted welcome signs at each end of Main Street. These colorful wooden signs were created by Janice Hemphill. Selling buttons designed by artist Nan Keenan was a fundraiser for the project. The buttons featured three commemorative plants and were inspired by the reserved society in the 1850s, when people used flowers to express their feelings—a practice called florigraphy. County Executive Chuck Ecker distributed awards to participants in a ceremony at the Railroad Station Plaza in September.

Chapter 2

The Creation of Ellicott's Mills

The story of Ellicott City begins with the Ellicotts—a father and son, both named Andrew—who came to Bucks County, Pennsylvania, from Devonshire, England, in 1730. The following year the son married Ann Bye, daughter of a well-established landowner. The couple had five sons: Joseph, John, Andrew, Nathaniel and Thomas. The oldest, Joseph, returned to England in 1766, sailing on the ship *Hibernia* out of Philadelphia to claim his great-grandfather's estate in Collumpton. The proceeds of £1,500 sterling provided the capital that he and his brothers needed to buy the land in Maryland for their mill venture.

Three of the Ellicott brothers—Joseph, John and Andrew—came to Maryland from Pennsylvania. The Ellicotts bought land on both sides of the Patapsco River, totaling two miles along the shores in either direction from the mill area, in keeping with a 1669 Maryland law that permitted anyone who built a mill to have up to twenty acres of land on either side of the river and to hold it for eighty years. They paid three dollars per acre for eight hundred acres. The ample water power of the Patapsco would be enough to run their proposed gristmills. In May 1771, they brought their equipment to the Lower Mills.

By the end of 1774, just prior to the Revolutionary War, they had cleared the land, built and were operating a mill one hundred feet long and built a large log building for housing for the millworkers. Ellicott's Lower Mills became one of the largest settlements in the colonies, with a mill, dam, millrace and workers' housing.

The Ellicotts believed in the financial viability of grain over tobacco as the crop of choice and planted their own crops. They were also the first to introduce commercial fertilizers to Maryland, teaching farmers to replenish the soil with plaster of Paris.

The Ellicotts invented the elevator and hopper boy used in flour mills but didn't patent their inventions. Rather, they invited others to apply the technology to their own mills. The brothers were very resourceful. There was no road to Baltimore from Ellicott's Mills, so the Ellicotts built one at their own expense. The road ended at the harbor in Baltimore, where the brothers built a wharf and warehouses to accommodate the exportation of their flour. The Ellicotts built their wharf in 1783, when New York was still occupied by the British army. They extended their wharf on Light Street by dredging the sediment from the bottom of the harbor to accommodate oceangoing vessels. John Ellicott rode ten miles to Baltimore daily to purchase wheat and sell flour, thus becoming the first merchant miller. In 1797, with his brothers, Jonathan Ellicott, son of Andrew and Elizabeth, planned the road from Baltimore to Frederick, Maryland. George surveyed the route at the age of seventeen. It was the first road of its kind in Maryland—the beginning of the National Road.

In July 2000, the Maryland State Highway Administration selected the historic district of Ellicott City as the site for the kickoff event for its new Scenic Byways Program. Maryland designated thirty-one scenic byways across the state to reflect Maryland's environmental, historic and cultural destinations. Ellicott City's Main Street represents the historic National Road.

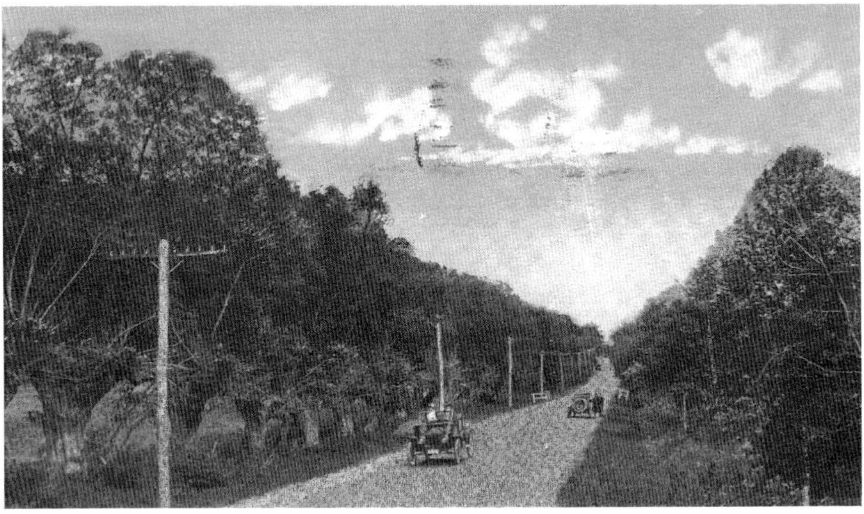

A part of the National Road. *Courtesy of Victoria Goeller.*

CHARLES CARROLL OF CARROLLTON

One of the wealthiest men in the colonies, Charles Carroll of Carrollton lived west of the Ellicott's Mills settlement at Doughoregan Manor, an estate of over thirteen thousand acres that he inherited from his grandfather, Charles Carroll the Settler, who had acquired it in 1702. Carroll of Carrollton was one of four Maryland signers of the Declaration of Independence, the only Catholic and the last to die. He believed in the Ellicott brothers and their vision and, following their example, had grain planted on his property, with substantial profit. With this model, local farmers soon followed suit, and the area became a premier milling site. Charles Carroll also encouraged local farmers to plant wheat by lending them the money to do so, making him one of the few bankers in the area.

While Charles Carroll lived at Doughoregan, distinguished visitors included George Washington, Thomas Jefferson, John Hancock, Benjamin Franklin and James Monroe. The mansion, of national importance, is unique in that it has been in the Carroll family for its entire existence, up to the present time. Charles Carroll is buried in the chapel located on the property. The Carroll family is considering the sale of a portion of the estate for senior housing and donating another portion to the county for athletic fields. The owners of Doughoregan hope to keep intact the final, approximately six-hundred-acre property.

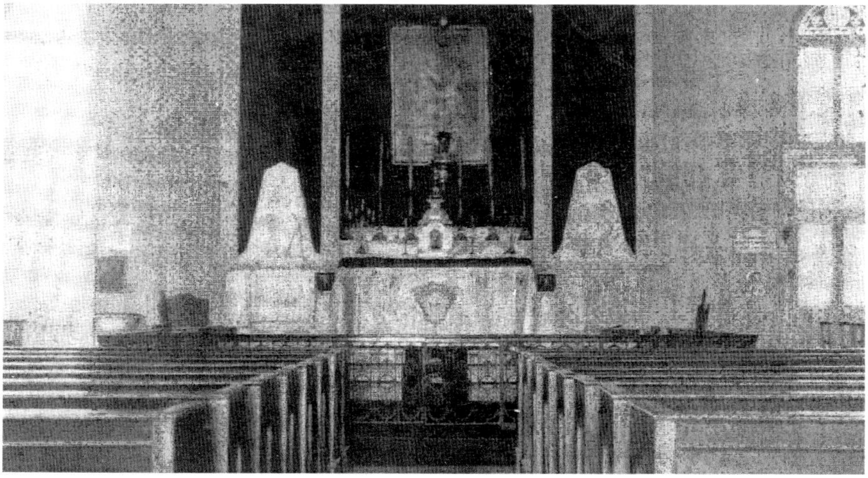

Doughoregan Chapel. *Courtesy of Victoria Goeller.*

George and Jonathan Ellicott

George Ellicott and his brother Jonathan built large stone houses next to the Patapsco Mills, where they lived for over forty years. The still-standing George Ellicott House was built in 1789. The families were very social, and friends and neighbors often visited. In her book, *The Settlement of Ellicott's Mills*, George's daughter Martha describes the visit of Little Turtle and other Indian chiefs to her father's home during Christmas week in 1807. Martha was twelve years old when the visit occurred. The Native Americans were returning home after a visit to Washington, D.C., and stayed overnight at an Ellicott City hotel with United States agent William Wells as interpreter. They included Little Turtle and Rusheville, chiefs of the Miami nation; Beaver and Crow of the Delawares; two Shawanese chiefs; and the Raven, chief of the Potowatomies. George Ellicott visited them at their hotel in Ellicott's Mills and invited them to his home for dinner. One Native American visitor dressed in a bearskin with claws and teeth attached and wore a painted face, but the rest wore waistcoats and pantaloons similar to what the colonists wore at the time. Out of deference to the guests, one of the dishes served was hominy.

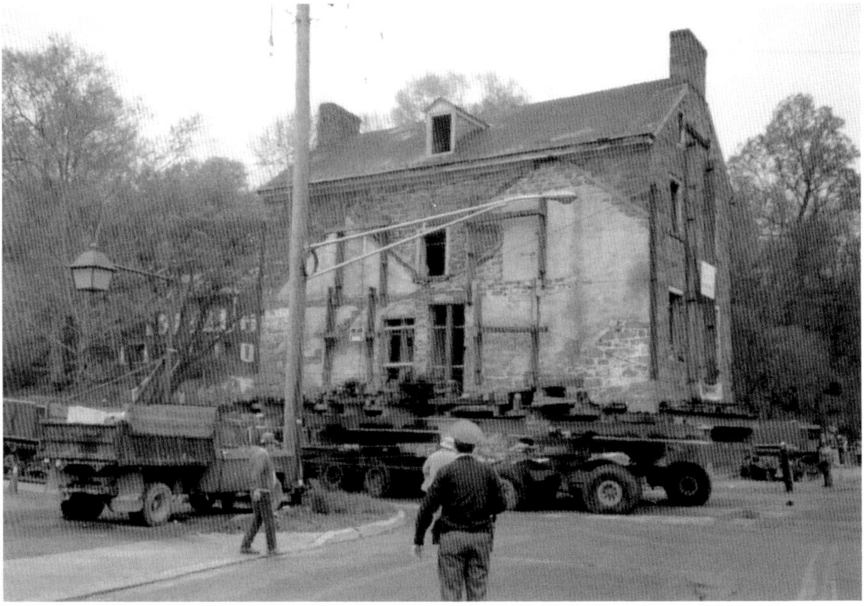

Moving the George Ellicott House. *Courtesy of Victoria Goeller.*

Jonathan took over management of the Patapsco Mills in 1812. For almost two hundred years, the George Ellicott House survived in its location near the mill, next to Jonathan's house. Jonathan's house was destroyed by Tropical Storm Agnes in 1972, and George's home was badly damaged by Tropical Storm Eloise in 1975. The current mill owners, the Wilkins-Rogers Company, owned the house and had planned to restore it until Eloise caused the collapse of a corner of the building. Preservationists intervened and Wilkins-Rogers gave the house to them. This led to an ambitious plan to move the house to a safer, higher-level location on the other side of Frederick Road. It cost over $1 million to move and restore the house. A partnership of Historic Ellicott City, Inc., Judge John L. Clark, Senator James Clark and Charles Wagandt's Oella Company enabled the move, made on April 25, 1987. For the move, specialists placed the house on steel beams on a large truck and carefully moved it across Frederick Road. The restoration was completed in 1991, and the building now contains elegant office space.

The last direct descendant of the original three Ellicott brothers living in Howard County died in 1964 at the age of eighty-four. He was Frank Ellicott, a descendant of Andrew Ellicott. George Ellicott, the great-grandson of Andrew, married Kate Duvall and raised eight children on his farm outside Ellicott City. Frank was the last survivor of the family and lived on the farm until his death.

Quaker Architecture

The Ellicotts completed a millrace in 1774, after two years of construction. In 1789, John Ellicott, son of the founder John, used the millrace to demonstrate a steam-propelled boat that he had built. He accidentally lost his arm during an explosion of the steam boiler onboard his boat and so did not proceed, or else he may have beaten Fulton to the discovery by a few years. Robert Fulton designed and built the Clermont, the first commercially successful steamboat, in 1807. On June 26, 1940, the State Roads Commission, employing Work Projects Administration (WPA) labor, began the work of filling in the millrace to accommodate a wider highway.

The Ellicott brothers were Quakers, and when they migrated to this area from Pennsylvania, other Quakers joined them. They were skilled in stonemasonry and carpentry, and they applied their crafts to building homes as well as mills. The Quakers simplified the Federal style of architecture

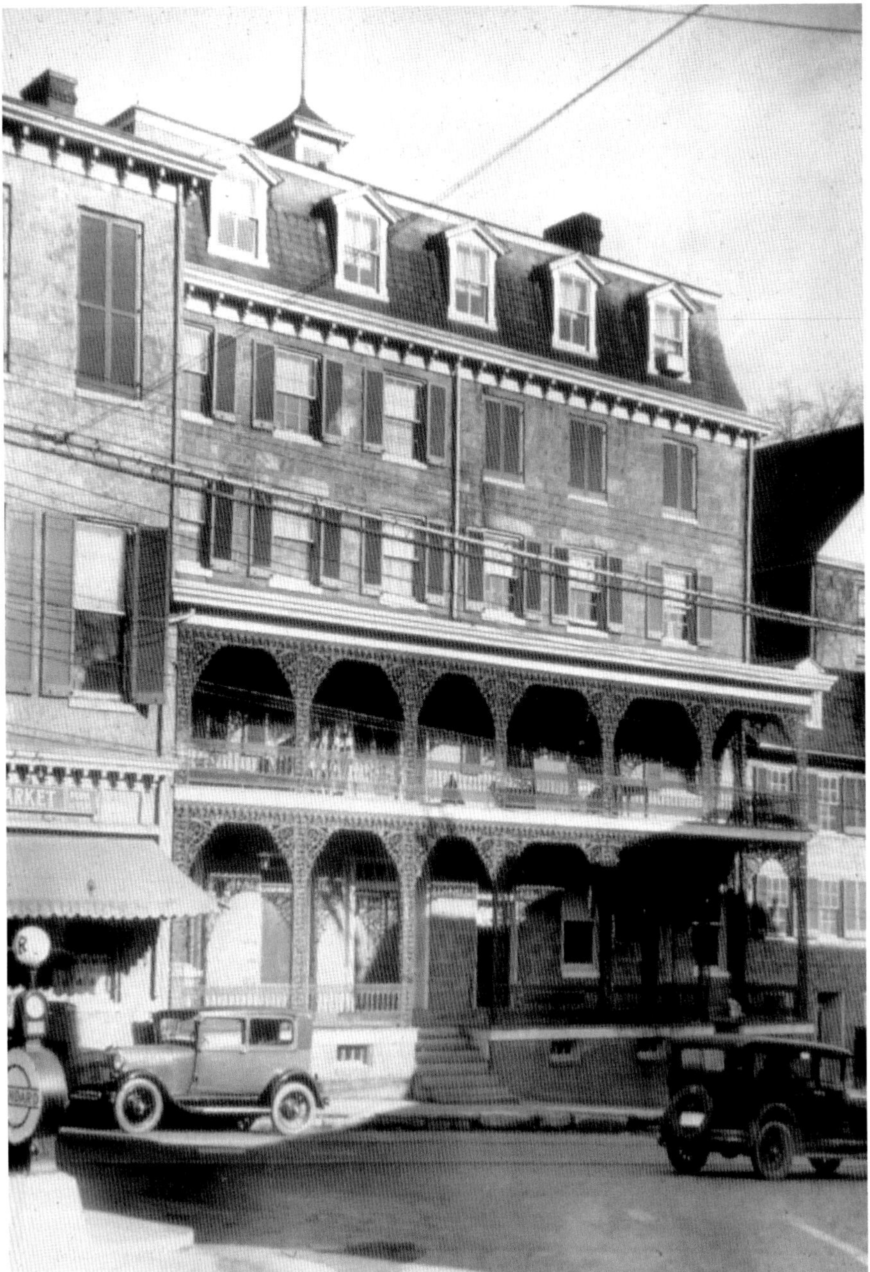

The Howard House. *Courtesy of Herb Johl.*

favored at the time, neoclassical in origin and popularized in the United States by Thomas Jefferson. The Quakers were plain in taste as well as religion. They used local materials including wood, granite and rubble stone, and much of the town can be described as early eighteenth-century mill town style.

A typical example, Hill House, near the corner of Hill and Main Streets, is a four-level granite house built in 1838. In the 1990s, the owner did extensive research at the Howard County Historical Society to determine this date, contrary to the 1824 date engraved on a plaque at the front gate. One of the earliest dwellings built on the Mount Misery Land Patent, it was a parsonage in the 1860s—possibly home to the rector of Emory United Methodist Church. The first documented owner of the house was Walter Brown, a gentleman farmer who owned additional land farther down Frederick Road in Baltimore County. Brown is listed in property records as an owner in March 1838.

An inventory of the estate of Walter's son, Richard, made in 1859 named the rooms in the house. The ground floor featured an ironing room and a dining room. The second floor included a front parlor and a back parlor. The third floor was divided into front chamber, back chamber and end chamber, while the fourth-floor attic included a front and end chamber. A wooden addition on the south side of the house held the kitchen and an office.

In 1968, after the house had stood vacant for twenty-five years, a new owner, Diane Shulte, bought it as a shell with no heat and no roof. Scavenger hunts to demolition projects provided the stone and brick used to reconstruct the house and gardens. The owner added original King George IV door latches, made in England, as well as cherry paneling and chestnut crown molding in the dining room. The house evolved into a showplace regularly featured in the Maryland House and Garden Pilgrimage and the Howard County Historical Society's Annual Christmas Candlelight Tour. In 1976, the Howard County Bicentennial Commission declared the house a "Designated Landmark" property.

INTERVIEW WITH EARL KLEMM

Earl Klemm lived in Hill House from 1995 to 1998:

> *When we bought the house from Diane Shulte it was in good shape. We did replace the heat, air conditioning and roof and remodeled the kitchen. Diane*

came to visit one day and looked at the roof and remarked that it was the same one she had put on and it was still in good shape. That very night we had a storm—and a leak in the roof. Hill House is a hard house to live in. It looks very impressive from the outside, but inside there are lots of stairs. I think the house is haunted. We heard doors slam and sounds of furniture crashing. One time my cousin was in the dining room when a pen levitated and flew across the room. I like living in old houses—in 1998 I moved from Hill House to a Victorian farmhouse built in 1878, just up the street. Hill House was built before the Civil War. I like to wonder who walked through there, what did they think, what did they know?

In the early nineteenth century, several more imposing buildings were constructed in the Greek Revival style, including the Ellicott City Courthouse, the Patapsco Female Institute and Mount Ida, but they were still quite plain. A few of the early mill buildings have over time been decorated with Victorian gingerbread but most adhere to their Quaker simplicity. One of these is a former residence on upper Main Street, a well-done Victorian structure along the lines of the "Painted Ladies" of San Francisco and Cape May. Now business offices, its renovation won a nonresidential award in 1998 from the Historic District Commission.

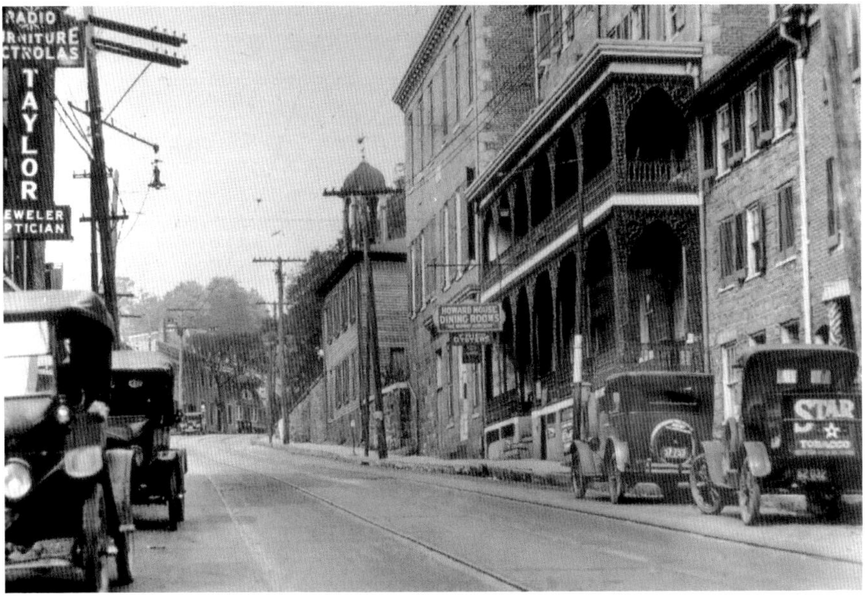

Looking west on Main Street. *Courtesy of Herb Johl.*

According to a report prepared by Jean Hannon in 1975, nominating Ellicott City for inclusion in the National Register of Historic Places, Ellicott City still had about 7 buildings built between 1700 and 1800; 110 buildings built between 1800 and 1850; 80 buildings built between 1850 and 1900; 60 buildings built between 1900 and 1950; and 12 buildings built between 1950 and the present. It is amazing that of the almost 200 buildings constructed before 1900, most were still serving useful functions in the community.

A GROWING MILL TOWN

Due to the availability of water power, others eventually built mills in the area. The proximity of this water had its downside, in the form of area flooding that over time has destroyed many of the old structures built along the riverbanks. There were seven mills in the area of what is now the historic district of Ellicott City. The most prominent location is the Ellicotts' grist- and sawmill, just east of the Patapsco River on Frederick Road. The Ellicotts lost the mill to the Union Bank of Maryland in 1841. The Great Flood of 1868 severely damaged it. In 1922, Morris Shapiro purchased the mill and renamed it the Continental Milling Company. This company made flour for the Doughnut Corporation of America, which purchased the building in 1926. During World War II, the mill was diversified to build radar equipment and gun parts. In 1967, the Wilkins-Rogers Company purchased the mill and still owns it. The company produces Washington-brand flour. It is the last commercial gristmill in Maryland.

The Atkinson oil and card mill was near Main Street and Columbia Pike, where Parking Lot D, behind the former post office, is now located. In 1804, Joseph Atkinson leased land from the Ellicotts and built oil and wool mills. A dam on the Tiber Branch of the river supplied the water source for both mills. Mill operations ceased around 1808. The buildings and dam no longer exist, but several former workers' homes still surround the parking lot.

Just west of Ellicott Mills Drive on Main Street stands the building that once housed the Burgess Mill. In 1823, George Burgess began operating a gristmill on the Hudson Branch of the Tiber River. Until 1906, the mill served as a gristmill for three months of the year and a wagon works the rest of the year. In 1917, Samuel W. Burgess opened a Buick dealership at the site. The county enclosed this branch of the river in the 1960s, making it much less visible. It now runs under several buildings on the north side of Main Street, then under Main Street and over to the south side, where it is visible in the former post office parking lot. The white wooden building formerly housing the mill now provides office space. The millrace can still be seen behind it. The Burgess family's brick home still stands on the hill overlooking the mill.

The Ellicotts' iron mill was located on the east bank of the Patapsco, north of Main Street. The Ellicotts built the mill in 1810 to make nails, wrought iron and copper utensils. It burned down in 1864 and was replaced by a cotton mill, which was destroyed by the flood of 1868.

In the heart of town, at the intersection of a cobblestone passageway and the Tiber River, is the site of the Hawes Grist Mill, also called the Depot Mill, in what is currently the Rumor Mill restaurant, formerly Side Streets restaurant. Old beams, flooring and granite walls are still visible in the building. A three-story gristmill was built on this site around 1850. The mill produced buckwheat flour. In 1891, Herman Shriver purchased this mill and converted it to the production of electricity, becoming the first electric light company in Ellicott City. Patapsco Power and Light bought the mill in 1904.

Interview with Becky Williams

Becky Williams has lifelong ties to Ellicott City and still visits often:

> *I was born in 1966 and lived in the historic district of Ellicott City from 1973 to 1981. We lived in the building that was once a mill and later became Side Streets restaurant. Before we moved in, the building was modified from a mill to a house. The wheel was gone—we used to play in the space where it was. In 1975, our house was flooded by Tropical Storm Eloise. The water filled the first floor and covered the bridge right next to our house. I remember seeing a woman walking along and holding up her blouse so it wouldn't get wet, which I thought was pretty strange. We sat on top of the garage and watched people walking by and then boats, too. The mud was the worst part. My brother's friends from high school came over and helped us clean up. The house was gutted and redone after the flood. There was a hole in the wall by the stream, and it was used to move materials from the boats that came up the stream.*

I remember Mr. Bibo owned the building across the street and let me play there. That's the Forget-Me-Not Factory now. I remember Cate Olsen and her shop, the Owl and the Pussycat, and the pottery she sold. The store owners all knew me. I did odd jobs up and down Main Street as a child. I was a "go-fer." I'd go door to door to see what shop owners wanted for lunch and then I'd go to the deli and get it for them.

Cate Olsen led a lot of events in town. I remember her bringing breakfast muffins to Miss Odette [Tersiguel] *in the morning. One of my favorite events was the May Flower Fest. When I was seven or eight, I was named "Miss Ellicott City" as part of this event. They had a parade, closed off Main Street and I rode through the town in a carriage, my hair in pigtails. They had waiters' races and other activities. I was depressed when they ended the May Fests.*

When I was eleven years old I went to work as a coat-check girl at Chez Fernand. I remember we all laughed when a patron shared that "me and Chez go way back." I learned to parallel park on Main Street and took ballet classes at Caryl Maxwell's. Sometimes my father would give me ten cents, and I'd go to Mr. Ray's grocery store and buy Charleston Chews. One time Mr. Ray said that the candy now cost fifteen cents. I asked why and he said, "Inflation." So I went home and asked my father for five more cents. He asked what for, and I said, "Inflation." Mr. Ray was the best. I also liked RC Cola from him—I decided the drink was named after me, as my maiden name was Rebecca Cannon.

I went to Ellicott City Elementary School. I remember Field Day one year. I had a one-line part in a play about Columbus discovering America. The scenery included a large boat. I walked into the boat and hit my head and wasn't able to say my line. One time when there were lines to sign up for things, I got in the wrong line and ended up playing the violin for five years as a result. Then when I got to high school they didn't have violin, so I signed up for art, and now all these years later I'm an art teacher, so everything worked out okay.

MEASURING TIME

About three miles outside of the historic district, Joseph Ellicott built Ellicott's Upper Mills. Benjamin Hood founded this site in 1766, and the area was known as "Hood's Haven." In 1774, Joseph Ellicott left Ellicott's Lower

Mills and purchased the milling operation from the Hood family. Joseph managed the Upper Mills, while Andrew and John remained with the Lower Mills. In 1775, Joseph constructed a three-story house for his large family. Northwest of the mill, the home was one of the first to have running water supplied by nearby springs. The estate, known as Fountainville, included rare ornamental flower gardens, a fish pond and a fountain. The house had a large entrance hall to accommodate the musical clock that he constructed in 1769. Joseph had studied the basics of clockmaking in England, but this clock was different from any other in existence at the time. It was eight feet high, and all four mahogany sides were finished, as the clock was designed to sit in the middle of the room. One face featured the sun, moon, earth and planets all moving in their orbits. A second face showed seconds, minutes, hours, days, months and years, with hands pointing to the correct time. A third face played twenty-four songs popular before the American Revolution. A pointer in the middle could be directed at a tune and it would play. The fourth face was clear glass so people could see the inner workings. His was not the only notable clock in the area over the years. Another was made by Benjamin Banneker, who became well known in the area when in 1753, at

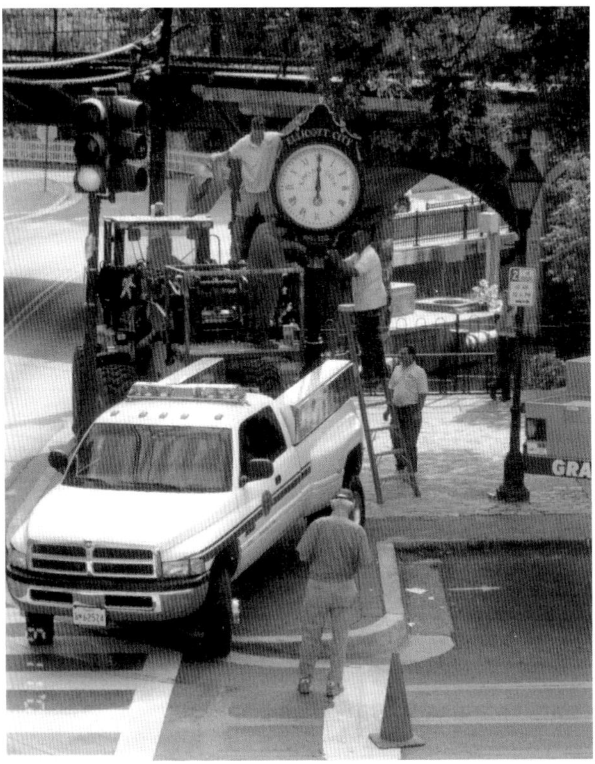

The clock installation in the Railroad Plaza. Courtesy *Courtesy of Victoria Goeller.*

the age of twenty-two, he created a wooden striking clock using a pocket watch as a model.

The newest notable clock was one erected in 2001 in honor of Howard County's Sesquicentennial, a celebration of its 150 years as a county. On June 16, 2001, the town celebrated the dedication of this new town landmark—the clock at the Railroad Plaza. The clock is a gift to the town from the Kiwanis Club of Ellicott City in honor of the county's Sesquicentennial and the club's sixtieth birthday. The replica is fifteen feet, four inches tall. The clock's timekeeping is monitored by satellite. To place the clock, the cobblestones paving the plaza were carefully removed, numbered and replaced in order. Workers digging the base discovered water four feet down, which altered plans for securing the clock. Today it serves as an excellent meeting place—and timepiece—for tourists and locals alike.

BENJAMIN BANNEKER

Benjamin Banneker, an African American, was a member of the Ellicotts' circle of friends. He was a man with a strong quest for knowledge and of great intelligence—attested to by his work in astronomy and mathematics. Banneker was born on November 9, 1731, the grandson of an English woman and a Senegalese prince who was her slave before they married. Their oldest daughter, Mary, married a freed slave named Robert in 1730. Typical of the time, Robert had no last name, so the couple adopted the name Banneky (later changed to Banneker). Robert and Mary had five children—Benjamin (the oldest), sisters Minta, Jemima and Molly and brother Julian.

In 1737, when Benjamin was six years old, his father purchased one hundred acres known as "Stout" from Richard Gist. The Bannekers were one of the first free black families to own property in the area. Benjamin was listed on the deed as the co-owner, possibly to ensure his eventual inheritance of the land.

Banneker, who never married, assumed management of the farm upon the death of his father on July 10, 1759.

There was great change in the valley and in Banneker's life when the Ellicott brothers arrived in 1772 and began construction of their gristmill. The Ellicotts contracted with the Bannekers for the purchase of poultry, fruits, vegetables and honey for their workers. Benjamin visited the mill, and the Bannekers were among the first customers of the Ellicott's Mills store, where their purchases included salt, chocolate and rum.

Sparked by a shared interest in science and nature, a friendship grew between Banneker and George Ellicott. Ellicott lent Banneker astronomy texts and simple instruments that Banneker used to produce an ephemeris (a table of computed positions of celestial bodies), which he unsuccessfully attempted to have published in 1791. Major Andrew Ellicott, Joseph's son, had worked with James Madison to extend the survey of the Mason-Dixon line in 1784. In 1791, Benjamin Franklin recommended Andrew, and George Washington selected him to survey Washington, D.C., to finish the work begun there by Pierre Charles L'Enfant. In turn, Andrew chose Banneker as an assistant. Banneker traveled to Washington and cared for Ellicott's surveying and astronomical instruments. The following year, with assistance from the Ellicotts, Banneker had an ephemeris published in the form of an almanac. It included weather forecasts, advice for farmers and Banneker's writings.

Benjamin Banneker died at his home on October 9, 1806. On the day of his funeral, October 11, his home burned to the ground and many of his personal belongings were lost. In 1985, archaeological investigations uncovered the site of the Banneker homestead. Today, Benjamin Banneker Historic Park, which opened on his farmland on the east side of the Patapsco River in Oella on June 9, 1998, keeps his memory alive.

Chapter 3

The Railroad and the Town

The first trip by rail from Baltimore to Ellicott's Mills took place in August 1830, soon after the Baltimore & Ohio Railroad completed the track. The same year, Peter Cooper designed and built the Tom Thumb, the first American steam locomotive to travel on a commercial line. He built it to convince the owners of the B&O Railroad to use steam engines in their fledgling railroad. The Tom Thumb is best remembered for its race against a horse-drawn car on August 28, 1830.

The railroad had constructed two tracks between Baltimore and Ellicott's Mills, and the driver of the horse-drawn car on one track challenged the driver of the Tom Thumb on the second track to a race. The Tom Thumb easily led the race until a belt slipped off a pulley and the locomotive lost power, allowing the horse to win the race. This did not discourage the owners of the B&O, who soon after switched to steam locomotives. The first year it operated, the railroad carried over eighty-one thousand people.

There can only be one "Oldest Train Terminal in America" and Ellicott City has it—now a National Historic Landmark. In 1831, the Baltimore & Ohio Railroad constructed its first terminus in Ellicott City, on land donated by the Ellicotts. It is a substantial stone building, first built for freight but modified to accommodate passengers in 1857. It was designed by Jacob Small, a Baltimore builder. The superintendent of construction was Caspar Weaver. Samuel Smith served as the first agent for the depot and earned $400 per year.

Without benefit of modern equipment, craftsmen maneuvered massive granite blocks, quarried locally, and huge wooden beams to create a structure

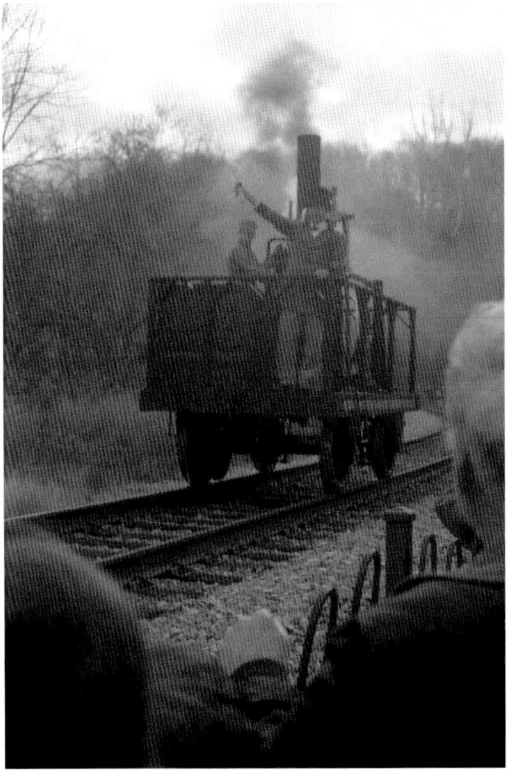

A replica of the Tom Thumb. *Courtesy of Victoria Goeller.*

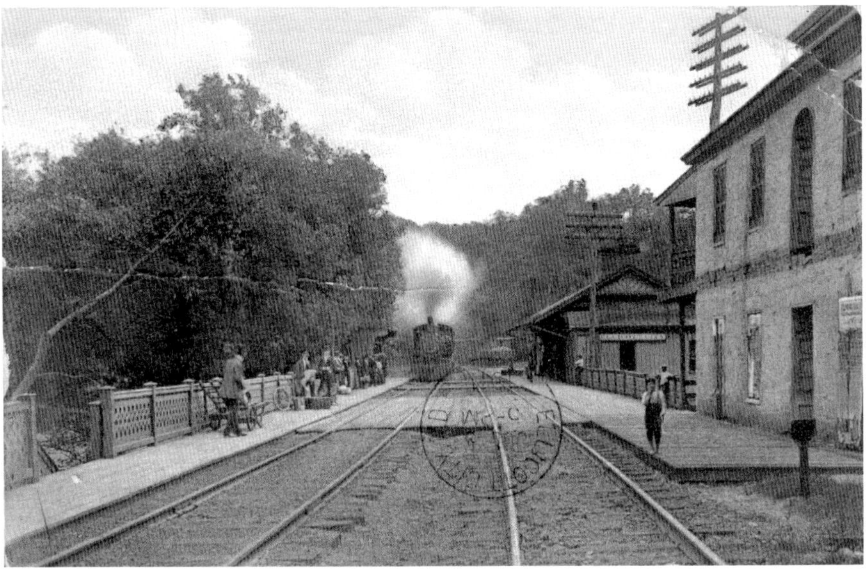

Double railroad tracks next to the Ellicott City B&O Railroad Station. *Courtesy of Victoria Goeller.*

that has lasted for nearly two centuries. The Ellicotts allowed the B&O to quarry granite for the construction of the building and the adjacent bridge from their quarries at no cost. The presence of this terminus meant that the cost of shipping goods to Baltimore was greatly reduced. When the railroad line continued farther west, Ellicott's Mills was a place where the trains stopped for meals. By the 1850s, many people traveled to the area by train to escape the summer heat of the city. Passenger service was discontinued in 1949. In 1968, through the efforts of Doris Thompson and others, the railroad station was declared a National Historic Building by the National Park Service. Freight service continued until 1972, when the facility was badly damaged by Tropical Storm Agnes. The Chessie System, which owned the station, considered demolishing it, but in an effort to save it, Historic Ellicott City, Inc. and the Howard County government combined their resources. The Chessie System leased the buildings to Howard County for one dollar per year, and Howard County signed an agreement with Historic Ellicott City, Inc. to work on the restoration of the buildings. Historic Ellicott City, Inc. coordinated a restoration effort using public and private funds of about $2 million.

IRISH LABORERS

In the pre–Civil War 1850s, the railroad was expanding westward, and bridges and tracks needed constant repair and maintenance. Irish, German and African American railroad workers came through Ellicott City. There was a lot of animosity among them as they were all competing for the same jobs—as well as animosity among the Irish themselves who represented different clans. Working conditions were dismal, with pay around fifty cents per day.

Today, one of the truly unique aspects of the historic district is that every now and then—more often than not on good weather weekends—you will be sharing the sidewalk with reenactors engaged in first-person impressions. This means that they will stay in character and answer questions in the context of the period they represent. One group that has been particularly popular is the Irish Laborers, which originated at the B&O Railroad Museum, Ellicott City Station, as part of the "Early Railroad History" program but branched out all over town.

When the group was in town, the members walked along Main Street, visited the shops, ate at restaurants like Tersiguel's and the Ellicott Mills

Brewing Company and offered impassioned speeches from the balcony of Ellicott's Country Store. Although the Ellicott City part of the railroad track was already completed when the majority of the Irish immigrated to America during the mid-nineteenth-century potato famine, they were still frequent visitors to the area.

Faith

There were few Catholics among the earliest settlers of the area, but with the railroad came an influx of traditionally Catholic German and Irish workers. Originally, Catholics went to Mass at the chapel in Doughoregan Manor. Soon, though, a church was built in the historic district. With its distinctive spire rising on Mulligan Hill, St. Paul's Roman Catholic Church is over 170 years old, built in 1838, just a few years after the Railroad Terminal. Like many other buildings in the historic district, the church was built on land formerly owned by the Quaker Ellicotts and sold to the church for a nominal five dollars. It is built out of granite from a local quarry—the same granite used in the steps of the Capitol in Washington, D.C. This is the church where George "Babe" Ruth married his first wife, Helen Woodford, in 1914, early in his baseball career.

Located appropriately on Church Road, Emory Methodist Church is one of the oldest churches in continual use in the historic district, established nearly a quarter of a century before the Civil War. In 1997, it made history when Reverend L. Katherine Moore became the first female pastor. Reverend Moore has worked hard to keep the small congregation (under two hundred people) active and involved. She has initiated children's ministries and an active youth group for teens.

In the 1870s, the Thomas Isaac Log Cabin on Merryman Street served as a mission for St. Luke's AME Church. In 1889, the church was founded in its present location on Main Street and became known as the "Friendly Little Church on the Hill." Parishioners have to climb a steep hill to access the church. Originally, the steps were wooden. After World War II, these were replaced with cement. As the years passed, the ground shifted and the steps became treacherous, unusable to senior and disabled church members. Besides obvious safety issues, the church members were concerned about presenting an attractive front to the community. Efforts were hindered by the fact that at the turn of the twenty-first century, the congregation consisted of fewer than sixty people. In 2002, the "stairway to heaven" was replaced, the work done by a group of volunteers and initiated by Betsey McMillion, who worked at the Department of Public Works at the time. She worked with someone who volunteered with Christmas in April, who made that connection on behalf of the church. Partnering with the Ellicott City Rotary Club and the Sunrise Rotary of Ellicott City, the work began on April 27. While the old steps were being removed from the eastern side, ground was broken for new steps, sturdy and including a hand rail, on the western side of the property.

RAILROAD STATION LEDGERS: INTERVIEW WITH HERB JOHL

"I moved to Maryland in 1954, from Wisconsin," said Herb Johl.

> *I was serving in the army at the time. After living in Anne Arundel County for several years, my wife Jesselyn and I became two of the early settlers in the new town of Columbia, arriving in 1967. Because of my great interest in history, and in trains, I was delighted by the proximity of our new home to Historic Ellicott City, and my wife and I visited frequently in the late 1960s, before the changes made by Tropical Storm Agnes in 1972.*
>
> *An early tour of the railroad station fueled my interest, and in 1972 Bicentennial celebrations drew me to become more involved in the history of the town. I joined the Howard County Historical Society, and there I met Roland and Enalee Bounds, who encouraged me to join Historic Ellicott City, Inc. I did, and soon after was made a board member. I have served in every volunteer position in the organization over the years.*

While working at the Railroad Station Museum, Johl inventoried a group of old ledgers he found in the attic during a restoration project. The ledgers include "Freight Received" in 1880 and 1881 and "Daily Bills for Manifest Received" from 1873 to 1882. In a ledger from 1876, there were instructions on how to make a copy of a document—a far cry from the Xerox machines and scanners of today:

> *Mann's Parchment Copying Paper—*
> *Directions for Copying*

Place a piece of blotting board under the leaf of copying paper; then, with a soft brush, wet the leaf. Brush in the surplus water with the hand; then place the written letter on the leaf (leaving the blotting paper under the leaf, to take up any excess water that may yet remain), place it in the press, and in ten or fifteen seconds a perfect copy will be secured.

The leaves WILL DRY AS SMOOTH AS SILK by placing the book in the press after copying.

Place the oil sheets between the copies just made, to prevent blending or setting off.

Johl shared a few letters that had been copied by this process:

January 12, (18)78
Ellicott City
Dec. 11 (187)6

N. Guilford, Esq.
GFA
Sir

I have three (3) bags Peruvian Guano in Warehouse left here during fall of 1876 by Gray Conductor Paul who reported the matter to agt at Camden, but so far has not heard anything from Agt about them and has found no owner for them on line of road.

Bags have no direction on them.

What disposition shall we make of them?

Respectfully,
C.W. Harvey, Agt

And:

Ell(icott) City
Jany 24 (186)7

Thos R Sharp Esq.
M of T
Sir

Mrs. Judge Mellor signals me to ask you if any arrangements can be made so that Judge Oliver Mellor can leave Annapolis on last train p.m. and connect at Relay Station with No. 20 for this place.

If President Biands would start his No. 5- at 4 instead of 4:20 p.m. it would enable the Judge to connect at Relay Station with No. 20 reaching here at 5:55 p.m.

Please do the best you can for them.

Respectfully,
C.W. Harvey Agt

RESTORING THE OLDEST RAILROAD TERMINAL: MEMORIES OF HERB JOHL AND RONALD BUCHMAN

"The late 1970s and the 1980s were a great time in the organization," remembered Herb Johl. "We worked at the station and we had a lot of fun. We did things like have a ball right inside Caplan's Department Store on Main Street. There were train trips, like one to Camden Station for dancing. We had a party at Lexington Market one time, called the 'Cabbages and Kings Ball.' In 1974, Enalee Bounds started the *Heritage* and I wrote for it for many years."

In 1974, major restoration work was done at the station, and a new slate roof was installed. Volunteers and students from Catonsville Community College conducted an archaeological dig at the turntable site and uncovered the original 1863 turntable pivot stone. The group reopened the facility as a museum in 1976, in time to celebrate America's Bicentennial.

"In August of 1976, the Ellicott City B&O Railroad Station Museum opened to the public after its first major restoration," Johl continued.

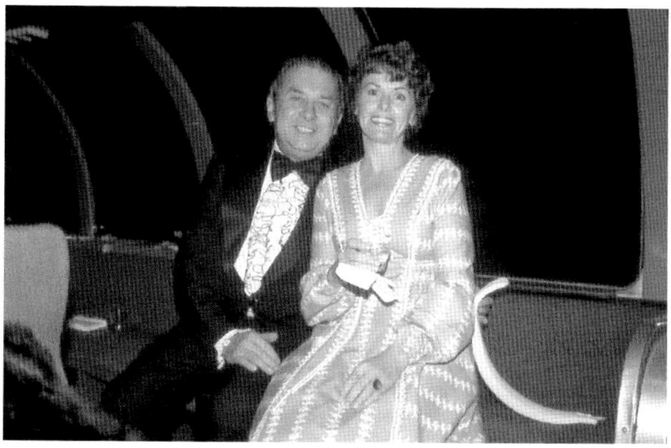

Herb and Jesselyn Johl in a train on the way to Camden Station. *Courtesy of Historic Ellicott City, Inc.*

I remember the yellow caboose being delivered. It was an amazing sight. In the fall of 1977, we had a program at the Railroad Station called "Lanterns and Leaves." The station was open at night, lit only by lanterns, and drama students put on skits for the entertainment of visitors. In 1978, the museum received a historical preservation award, and the historic district achieved National Historic Register status. One of the more unusual group tours took place in October of 1979—at 3:00 a.m. It was organized by a group that specialized in "insomniac's tours" and featured a visit to the station followed by breakfast at Chez Fernand. In 1980, a Tom Thumb replica came to the station, to the delight of hundreds of spectators. The event was attended by a variety of dignitaries, and a cake decorated with the image of the Tom Thumb was served. By 1983, the caboose was fully restored and painted red. It was used for children's parties and on August 20, 1983, a wedding was held there.

When the slate roof on the station building had to be replaced, the slates that were removed were stored at Jean Hannon's house. The group hoped to use them as a fundraiser, but that never worked out. We had a special exhibit at the station in 1984—Baltimore mayor William Donald Schaeffer's childhood trains. In 1990, Schaeffer sponsored a program called "Main Street Maryland," which brought passenger cars out of Baltimore for rides between Ellicott City and Sykesville.

On November 9, 1996, the Tom Thumb replica returned to the station, under steam, for a ceremony in which Chessie System Xtra (CSX, formerly Chessie) turned the deed for the railroad station over to the Howard County government for ten dollars.

In 1999, Historic Ellicott City, Inc. undertook the second major restoration of the Railroad Station Museum, which won the 1999 Preservation Project Award from the Maryland Historical Trust. This restoration returned the station to the way it looked in the late 1800s. The building was also made totally handicapped accessible, which led to an award from the Howard County Department of Citizen Services and Commission on Disability Issues in October 2000. The changes allow the museum to more fully tell the story of the station's place in local history, with living historians replicating the Patapsco Guard and the Fife and Drum section.

The Oliver Viaduct—the bridge next to the railroad station that carries trains over Main Street—was built at the same time as the station building. Originally designed with three stone arches for support, at the turn of the twentieth century two of the arches were removed to accommodate traffic on Main Street, being replaced by an iron bridge. In September 2003, the Oliver Viaduct received a makeover at the hands of a hardy group of volunteers from the Howard County Fire Department. The leader of the project was firefighter Wendy McCord, who used to drive under the bridge every morning on her way to work and bemoan the graffiti-laden entrance to town. She designed the project, organized the work crew and navigated the requirements of the Historic District Commission.

The volunteers used large handmade cardboard stencils for the lettering for "Ellicott City" and added small banners in freehand saying "Welcome to" and "Established in 1772." McCord also signed the painting as the work of "Howard County Fire Department No. 2 the A shift." The work continued for three days, despite the constant threat of an impending hurricane, and the resulting metallic letters on a vintage red background continue to delight today.

In a turn of phrase unique to Maryland, the winter holiday season brings on a rash of model train exhibits—known locally as "Christmas gardens." One of the best in the area is at the B&O Museum, Ellicott City Station. A variety of displays is featured, the major one being set up in the Car House. Today, from Thanksgiving to the end of January, the room holds a magical display, towering up at least three levels, and the display changes

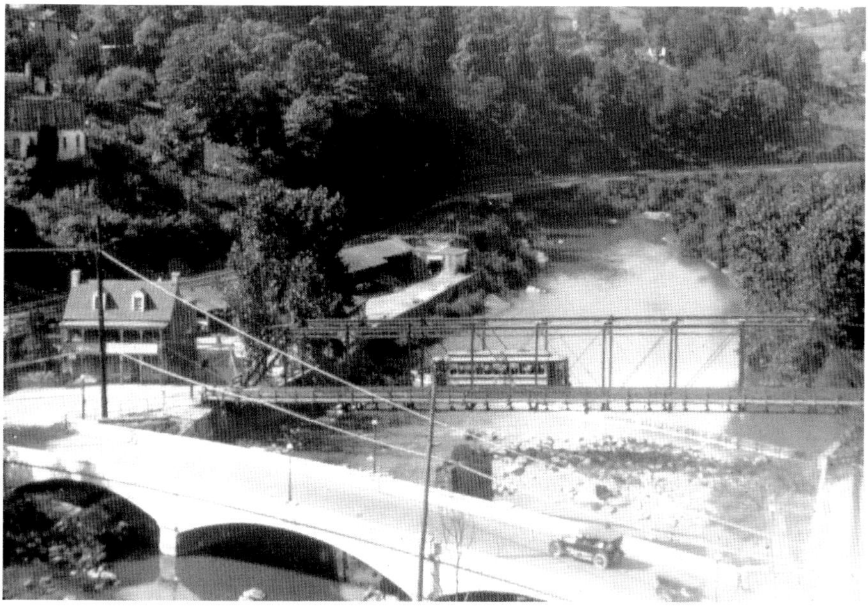

Aerial view of Patapsco River. *Courtesy of Herb Johl.*

every year. Volunteers take mountains of Styrofoam and carve them into intricate scenery, which is then sealed and painted. Vignettes usually found in the display include such features as logging camps, playgrounds, a carousel and, of course, trains. In keeping with the age of the museum building, the holidays usually provide a backdrop for reenactors enjoying a mid-nineteenth-century holiday at home. At that time, the stationmaster lived with his family in the station.

"As a tour guide on duty at the Station during the annual Christmas garden display in the '70s, I was approached by a man and woman as they were leaving," said museum volunteer Ronald Buchman. "They told me that they were disappointed in our display of only a few trees, greens and poinsettias, not the 'gardens' we had advertised. I detected an accent and asked where they were from and they replied Indiana, where what we in Maryland call Christmas gardens are simply train layouts. I've learned since that 'garden' is a very local term."

The Patapsco Guard

Howard County, like the rest of Maryland, was bitterly divided during the Civil War. Large landowners in the rural part of the county employed slave labor on their farms and plantations and were Southern sympathizers who enrolled in Confederate companies. The names of ninety-two Howard County men who fought for the Confederate army are listed on a bronze plaque on the lawn of the Howard County Courthouse in Ellicott City. There is no monument honoring Howard County soldiers who served in the Union army.

The majority of men in Ellicott's Mills were shopkeepers or millworkers. Although not indifferent to the outbreak of war, their allegiance was to their town and their livelihoods. In September 1861, Thomas McGowan proposed a local guard to protect Ellicott's Mills and the important B&O Station and its lines. Captain McGowan promised that recruits would remain home near their families and avoid combat.

Early on Sunday, July 10, 1864, alarmed residents of Ellicott's Mills heard the sound of the Union cavalry racing through town. Their only defense was the Home Guard, wounded veterans and men too old for war. Despite McGowan's promise, the Patapsco Guard was deployed elsewhere. But the Home Guard was not needed. Thousands of soldiers on foot, and wagons carrying the wounded from the Battle of Monocacy, arrived in town. One wagon halted in front of the Howard House, where soldiers unloaded four bodies. Residents buried the deceased soldiers in the cemetery on Quaker Hill without ceremony. As Main Street became clogged, people volunteered their homes and churches to serve as hospitals, and Ellicott's Mills citizens assisted the wounded and weary soldiers.

The Patapsco Guard Reenactors was created in the 1990s. "The popularity of the Civil War is a great way to interpret the importance of the railroad," said Jerry Talbert. "The Patapsco Guard used the enthusiasm of reenactors to create a presence outside the museum walls. The first year squads of soldiers were marching down Main Street, arresting 'Southern sympathizers' out of restaurants, firing volleys (after getting permission to discharge firearms in town) and calling attention to military and civilian life in that era."

"My son Dave joined the Patapsco Guard reenactors at the Ellicott City B&O Railroad Station Museum in 1994, just shy of his fourteenth birthday," Janet Kusterer recalled.

> *Dave elected to do this volunteering to fulfill his middle school requirement of offering time to the community. He quickly became immersed in the stringent requirements of the job: no eyeglasses unless they were period; no digital watches—pocket watches were the choice; scratchy wool clothing, even in summertime; and stiff shoes with thin soles. He was expected to tell museum visitors about military life in the 1860s and explain the importance of the railroad to the war effort. While he was too young to drive, I would pick him up after a day of volunteering. If he wasn't ready to leave, I would sit in the gift shop, on a seat that had been rescued from a vintage train car, covered in faded blue velvet upholstery.*

MEMORIES OF DAVE KUSTERER

"I was in the Patapsco Guard from the age of thirteen until the age of seventeen," said Dave Kusterer.

> *The Patapsco Guard was a military unit charged with defending the (almost) city of Ellicott's Mills from Confederate forces during the Civil War. I was not a member of the Patapsco Guard during the Civil War;*

my time came later, but it was the Patapsco Guard nonetheless, and I was a part of it.

My Patapsco Guard was charged with making sure that tourists at the Ellicott City B&O Railroad Museum had a good time and learned something from someone between the ages of thirteen and seventeen. A hard task on paper, and a harder one in person. We gave our all for the cause, though, showing up every weekend to wear what they would have worn during the period and dispense knowledge about the rooms in the museum. There were a few: there was the telegraph room, the freight agent's room, the waiting room, etc. I can't recall them all; it's too painful.

What kept me interested in being a member of the Patapsco Guard was the appeal of being a soldier in President Lincoln's army. This required extensive training in Federal army drill, and from time to time this training would draw us away from the museum for a weekend. I was learning.

One weekend training session involved a few guard members traveling to western Maryland to spend a weekend learning how to shoot blanks at fellow reenactors in the name of the cause. The attendee list was slim this weekend, as it was devoted simply to training and not to firing guns in anger at fat men in grey wool. I was excited for it, as were my friends and fellow travelers Danny and Patrick, and that was basically it. None of us had a license.

Guard member Dan Danielson was kind enough to feign excitement for this exercise, though. Better yet, he had a car. He agreed to pick us up from a central location on the morning of the first day of training and truck us out to whatever forgotten fort in semiwestern Maryland we were going to. He drove an Acura and had no answering machine. Great guy.

Danny, Patrick and I decided that in order to make the most of this training exercise, we had to be on the road bright and early Saturday morning. Being from disparate parts of the county, we figured we'd hole up at the museum Friday night, maybe watch a movie and drink whatever sherry was left in the displays and let Dan pick us up at one location in the morning. Ed Williams, who ran the museum at the time, saw no problem with the first part of this. The second part is embellishment a decade on but I'm sure I'm not far from my mindset. The third part eventually happened.

I'm a ghost guy. I like to think that they exist, and while I've never seen anything like what some people would call evidence that they're out there, I'm not convinced that they're not. In other words, I'm open. So are Danny and Patrick. We bug Ed for whatever ghost stories he's got about the museum. What he's got is dry and pretty stock: dragging chains, basically.

No fun. Still, we believe. We're recreating the past so surely the past is recreating itself and where better than here, the "Oldest Railroad Station in America"?

Ed gives us the keys to the joint (a big deal) and the code to the security keypad (a surprisingly lesser deal) and departs for the night. Ed, to this day, is co-owner of the Mumbles & Squeaks toy store on Main Street, so he's just going up there to sleep. If we need anything, he'll be probably two hundred yards away.

We come prepared for the evening. We decide to sleep in the freight agent's office, which is the only display room on the first floor of the museum. It's already got a bed in it, plus we have our bedrolls for the weekend. There are stairs in the room to the second, main, floor of the museum, and it's a room away from the front door of the place. We're separated from that by the gift shop. The gift shop has a little TV and VCR combo, and we brought a couple of movies to watch before going to bed. We moved it to where we were sleeping, laid out our rolls and watched Animal House. *I distinctly remember Danny insisting that I rewind Stork's only line in the movie so we could watch it again. We're in a good mood.*

That movie ends, and we're in no way tired because we are fifteen and we are on a sleepover. I—I think I had, maybe it was Danny—had brought Pulp Fiction *to watch, and I think that dates me and this piece just as well as it should. In fact, I'm sure it was me. We're watching the film—three fifteen-year-olds (forgive me, Danny and Patrick, if I'm erring by a year either way)—and there's a point very early on in the movie where John Travolta opens a briefcase secured by a combination lock. It's pretty dramatic, and the shot of the briefcase's combination being entered is, for the film, careful: it goes six, six…a woman screams from the top of the staircase in the freight agent's office and Danny, Patrick and I jump off of the floor, scream ourselves, hop over the fence designed to keep tourists away from the exhibit, tear through the gift shop (me on an asleep leg) out the door, at which point we collect ourselves enough to lock the door and hand Patrick the key so that he could stand guard. He was the newest member, after all.*

Danny and I know that Ed likes to drink at Side Streets, so we head there. He's at the bar, along with Kathy, the owner's wife, and Adam, the bartender. We incoherently bring them up to speed and all are very concerned with what we just went through, though they are considerably less than shocked by our experience. All of us do a bit of a search of the museum but find nothing, and eventually we go to sleep. Dan picks us up the next morning and that's basically it.

It was, of course, Ed all along, with Kathy's help. They snuck in through the main doors on the second floor of the museum and stood at the top of the stairs while we watched the movie. They waited until a quiet part in the action and Kathy just let loose. We ran for the door, they ran for theirs and had probably been back at the bar for about thirty seconds when we came crashing in. If we had had the guts to go upstairs we would have caught them red-handed, but instead (to my recollection) it was a couple days before we found out the truth, at which point my mom became pretty upset with certain museum employees. I stuck around there for a few years after that and not once did I see a ghost.

Ghosts notwithstanding, the station has seen visitors from all over the world, including Annie Oakley, Charles Dickens and former Maryland governor William Donald Schaeffer. It is currently a museum, a site on the Civil War Discovery Trail and on the National Register of Historic Sites.

An Incorporated Town

The Howard District of Anne Arundel County was created on January 25, 1839, and Ellicott's Mills was the center of government. Over the next decade, the government approved and collected tax levies, constructed public schools and laid out election districts, but the Howard District was not individually represented in Annapolis.

The completion of the Ellicott City Courthouse in 1843, and great growth in the area, strengthened the desire for the creation of Howard as a separate county. On July 4, 1851, the Howard District of Anne Arundel officially became Howard County, named after John Eager Howard, a hero of the Continental army and fifth governor of Maryland.

Ellicott's Mills became known as Ellicott City, an incorporated town, in 1867, when it obtained a city charter. Presiding as the first mayor was George Ellicott, grandson of founder Andrew Ellicott. The charter empowered the mayor and council to "remove nuisances, to suppress gambling, to license public amusements." Laws were passed to keep the streets clean and outlaw profane language, gambling and public drunkenness. The population of Ellicott City in 1880 was 1,722 people.

In 1914, lawmakers adopted a new form of government and revised the boundaries of Ellicott City. As the only incorporated city in Howard

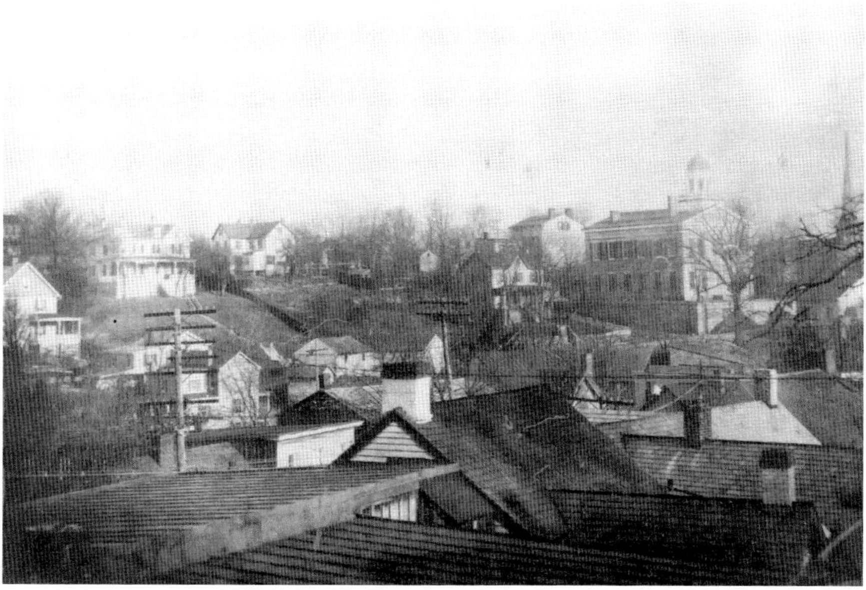

Bird's-eye view of town, including the Ellicott City Courthouse on top of the hill. *Courtesy of Victoria Goeller.*

County, Ellicott City was able to license the sale of hard liquor within its limits. As a result, saloons flourished. The city fathers collected high licensing fees from bar owners, thus creating a very low real estate tax base for property owners. With the start of Prohibition in 1920, compounded by the difficulties of the Depression, this windfall ended. After several years of bitter disputes, Senator Joseph L. Donovan introduced a bill to revoke the city's charter. The municipality faced bankruptcy, and at its request the Maryland legislature revoked its charter on July 1, 1935, and it came under county government rule.

HOWARD COUNTY'S 150TH BIRTHDAY PARTY

Howard County was born on the Fourth of July 1851, the second youngest county in Maryland. In 2001, the county celebrated its sesquicentennial—150 years of local history—with a year's worth of special events leading up to a grand finale. The celebration was the idea of former Howard County council member James Holway, who died before the event occurred.

County residents celebrated in many ways. There was a kickoff ceremony on July 4, 2000, featuring a band playing a specially written Sesquicentennial march and a traveling carillon. Local artist Joe Regan created a series of mural panels depicting scenes of historical interest from the nineteenth century. The panels were moveable and so were able to be displayed in a variety of places.

Another artistic undertaking was more grass roots. Called the "Pillars of the Community," these pillars were created by community groups, individuals, students and seniors who depicted the people, culture and traditions of the community. The Howard County Center for the Arts in Ellicott City displayed twenty-eight of the pillars, which ranged in size from six to eight feet high, as a group, and some continue to be displayed in venues around the county. Volunteers created the artwork in donated space in Columbia on a very limited budget. Planners expected only historic depictions on the pillars, but they got works depicting such varied topics as religious communities and the Columbia Archives as well.

Students of artist Bill Sachs created a work filled with familiar Ellicott City sites like the Quaker Meeting House, the Fire Museum, the old courthouse and Mount Ida. Local artist Alice Webb painted a pillar representing the home of Maryland state senator James Clark, Clarkland Farm. The pillar depicts Senator Clark in his trademark straw hat and suspenders riding a tractor. Volunteers from Historic Ellicott City, Inc. created a pillar that depicted trains, wheat and the Howard County colors. Organizers also delivered pillars to school art departments for decoration.

To further involve the kids along with the adults, the celebration committee came up with the concept of a *Passport to History*. This booklet featured drawings and write-ups about historic sites throughout the county, like the Thomas Isaac Log Cabin, the Patapsco Female Institute and the Railroad Station Museum in Ellicott City. People would visit the sites, where workers would stamp the book. When every site was stamped, the holder then turned in the booklet to be enrolled in a raffle. It was a nice way to learn local history. On the first "Passport Day," one couple succeeded in visiting all twelve sites to get their passports stamped by each—Herb and Jesse Johl. Although they had already visited all of the sites, they wanted to share in the excitement of the occasion.

Chapter 4

The Thriving Hub of Howard County

The Patapsco Female Institute is a majestic stabilized ruin that sits on one of the seven hills high above the town and features amazing views of the Patapsco River and the valley below. Designed by Robert Carey Long Jr. and built in 1837 as an academic school for young women, the eight-thousand-square-foot Greek Revival building features Doric columns and a classic façade. The Ellicott family donated seven of the acres that the building stands on. For many years in the mid-nineteenth century, young ladies aged twelve to eighteen from the finest families of the North and South lived at the school and studied music, languages, history and science.

Almira Hart Lincoln Phelps was principal from 1841 to 1856, and under her leadership the school flourished. She was considered a gifted teacher and wrote the first American teachers' manual for sciences. She also wrote many science textbooks that were used in schools in the nineteenth century. Almira pushed for high academic standards for her students, particularly to train highly qualified teachers.

The mothers of two women who almost became queens attended the school: Alice Montague Warfield, mother of Wallis Warfield, later the Duchess of Windsor, and Dorcas Spear Patterson, mother of Betsy Patterson Bonaparte, wife of Prince Jerome Bonaparte, who later became King of Westphalia. The Civil War disrupted the school and enrollment declined afterward. The school closed in 1891. One of the last principals was Sarah Randolph, great-granddaughter of Thomas Jefferson.

After the school closed, the building was used as a hotel—the Burg Alnwyck—a private residence, a World War I soldiers' convalescent hospital,

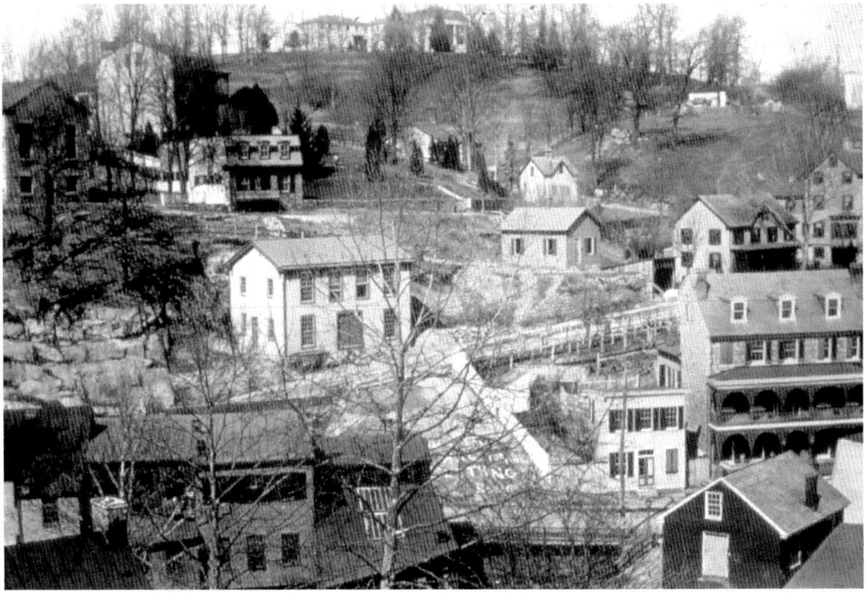

One of the seven hills of Ellicott City, with the Patapsco Female Institute on top. *Courtesy of Victoria Goeller.*

a home for the Hilltop Theatre and a nursing facility. After a period of disuse, the government of Howard County purchased the building in 1967 and placed it on the National Register of Historic Places in 1976. In cooperation with the Friends of the Patapsco Female Institute, the county stabilized the building and created a historic park and education center, which opened in 1995, thirty years after the Friends group was established. It is also the site of archaeological studies.

"I am very proud of the intervention done by Historic Ellicott City, Inc. that saved the Friends of the Patapsco Female Institute," said Herb Johl.

> *In the early years, the Friends of the Patapsco Female Institute were inactive and having membership problems. They had a treasury of about $3,000 or $4,000. Several persons that were members (they were members of Historic Ellicott City, Inc. also) attended one of our meetings and requested that their organization merge with Historic Ellicott City, Inc. After the proper paperwork was done, the Friends became part of us. We put their money in escrow and added to it with some of our fundraisers over the years. When the new Friends became active and obtained their 501(c)(3) status, we turned the escrow account, now about $12,000, over to them.*

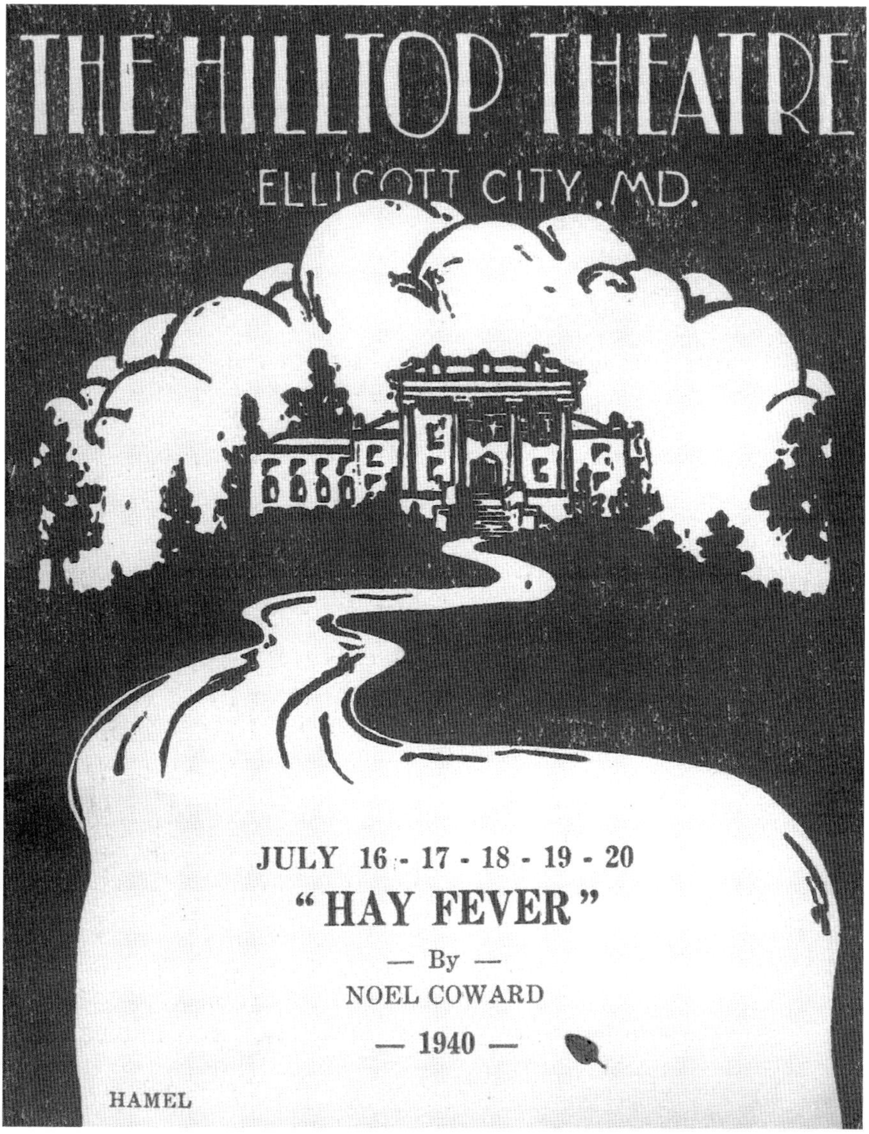

A Hilltop Theatre program. *Courtesy of Victoria Goeller.*

Today, Almira's Polite Society is named after the beloved former headmistress of the Patapsco Female Institute and celebrates Victorian activities for young ladies. One popular aspect of this group is the camps that they conduct throughout the year that range from one-day to one-week events. The camps are total immersion experiences for girls aged ten to twelve. They trade in their backpacks for pinafores to experience life in the nineteenth century.

The campers learn to use quill pens instead of laptops and to keep journals that are personalized with pressed leaves, newspaper clippings and drawings. They play Victorian parlor games, create craft projects like herbal beads to be strung into necklaces and learn about "current" events like the Mexican War, the gold rush and the Oregon Trail. They learn table manners, tea traditions, dancing and walking with books on their heads.

The Friends of the Patapsco Female Institute Historic Park continually works to find new and creative ways to make use of its dramatic site, including everything from Halloween ghost tours to weddings. One of the best has been the introduction of performances by the Chesapeake Shakespeare Company, billed as "Shakespeare in the Ruins." The company was formed in 2002, and in 2003 offered its first local production, *Romeo and Juliet*, directed by Ian Gallanar, at the outdoor site. The productions have been held yearly since, on weekends in June, and attendance has steadily grown. The productions are user-friendly, as the troupe wants to make Shakespeare accessible to all. Guests are entertained by a variety of small performances while waiting for the main event. One year the production schedule had to be adjusted to accommodate the arrival of the noisy seventeen-year locusts, which might have drowned out the actors with their nocturnal chirping, but otherwise the occasional shower is the only deterrent the group has encountered.

The Ellicott City Colored School, Restored

The Ellicott City Colored School was in operation from 1890 to 1953. It was later used as a church and then fell into ruin. The school, now restored, was built in 1888, a project approved by the Board of County Commissioners in 1879. Located on Frederick Road across from Rogers Avenue, the school is not the oldest segregated school for African Americans in Howard County, but it is the first built by the county. The school had a potbellied stove, desks with inkwells, outhouses and a staff of two who taught first through seventh grade. Although the Supreme Court outlawed segregation in 1954, it took Howard County eleven years to completely comply, eliminating one grade of segregated schooling a year. Sylvia Cooke Martin is the executive director of the Ellicott City Colored School restoration project. She became interested through her membership in the African American Historical and Genealogical Society. In 1989, fellow member Beulah Buchner discovered the ruin of the school hidden in brush while she was looking for a cemetery. Buchner worked hard to have the building restored.

The restoration project was led by the African American Historical Society, Howard County government and the Genealogical Society. Restorers had to replace a bridge to the parking lot, reinforce the hillside site, replace the stone foundation and replace the roof with a steeper one more in keeping with the original. Workmen used steel beams to reinforce the floors, shored bowed walls and built retaining walls along the perimeters of the property. An architectural historian provided oversight to ensure historical accuracy in the restoration, which cost about $1.4 million. It is now a museum and education center.

THE OLDEST STORE ON MAIN STREET

Twenty years after the end of the Civil War, Samuel J. Yates was operating a grocery store on Main Street. Yates Market is still in existence today, operated by Betty Yates Jacobs, the great-great-granddaughter of the store's founder. Betty's father, S. Bladen Yates, began working in his father Samuel I. Yates's store as a child of seven or eight. Bladen's first job was carrying vegetables in and out of the store. The store has an old meat box built into it that is still in use today. There's a door on top, and deliverymen would bring in hunks of ice twice a day and fill it to the top of the box. Later, Bladen's father had it changed to electric refrigeration. At one time, there were fifteen grocery stores on Main Street. Today, only Yates still exists. It has always been known for personal service and home delivery.

In 1937, at age nineteen, four years before he married his wife Ditty, Bladen opened S. Bladen Yates Hardware next door to the grocery store. During World War II, due to gas rationing, Yates brought back horse and wagon deliveries. As business warranted, Bladen Yates assumed the day-to-day running of the grocery, and the hardware store became Ditty's domain.

Yates Market is the last of its kind in the historic district, still custom cutting meats, making sage sausage from a secret family recipe, duplicating keys and caning chairs. After the death of Bladen Yates in 2002, his daughters, Betty Yates Jacobs and Cheryl Yates Libertini, consolidated the businesses, renting the former hardware store location next door to an antiques dealer. While old-fashioned, the grocery store offers modern amenities like gourmet

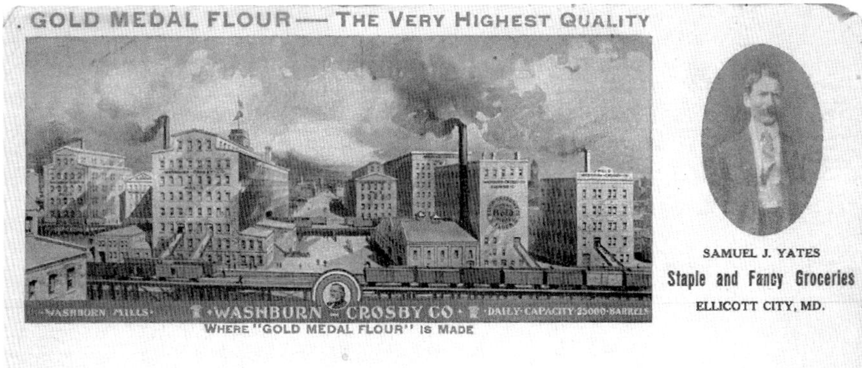

Samuel Yates's advertising postcard. *Courtesy of Historic Ellicott City, Inc.*

seafood, fresh turkeys and hams, cold sodas, freshly made sandwiches and an impressive candy selection. You can still get your groceries delivered, regular customers are welcomed by name and Betty Yates Jacobs, with the help of Earl Klemm, continues the tradition of personal service that has made Yates Market a landmark on Main Street for generations.

"Since 2000, I've worked at Yates Market," said Earl Klemm. "In this economy, it's great to live a three-block walk from work. People come to Yates for the Pfeffercorn coffee, fresh Thanksgiving turkeys and homemade sausage. I remember Bladen Yates well. He was a nice person, a true judge of character, a soft touch and a real baseball lover. In the short time I've been in Ellicott City, I've seen the movie theater leave, the firehouse, the bank and now the post office."

Interview with Cheryl Yates Libertini

Bladen Yates's older daughter, Cheryl Yates Libertini, related the following:

> *As a child I lived on Hill Street. My father and grandfather operated S.J. Yates and Sons Grocery, and my mother operated S. Bladen Yates Hardware. Eventually my family moved to a home my parents had built on Waterloo Road, next door to my grandfather, Samuel I. Yates. I attended Ellicott City Elementary School and graduated from Howard High School.*
>
> *We purchased everything on Main Street. If I needed socks, my mother would send me down the street to Caplan's. The saleslady would look at*

my foot, pick out a pair of socks and say, "These should fit." She would put the purchase on our account. My father, S. Bladen Yates, purchased my mother Dorothea's [Ditty] *Christmas present at Caplan's or Taylor's every year. He would wrap the gift in butcher paper and tie it with string. If I was sent on an errand down Main Street, I would be cautioned not to go anywhere else and to come right back. When I was growing up people thought lower Main Street was unsafe.*

I remember there was an agreement among several stores including Yates, Paul's Market, Valmas Brothers and Ray's Market to be closed on Wednesday afternoon. Eventually someone breeched the agreement; I think it was Paul's Market. Not wanting to miss out, all the stores began staying open on Wednesday afternoon.

INTERVIEW WITH GLADYS STANTON CROSS AND DEBBIE TEMPLE

"I am eighty-nine years old and have lived in the same house for seventy years, moving there as a teenaged bride in the 1930s," said Gladys Stanton Cross in 2004.

I live with my daughter Teressa in the house my husband was born in and where he died. Our next-door neighbors were Isaac and Rose Taylor, founders of Taylor Manor Hospital and Main Street property owners. My family donated the Thomas Isaac Log Cabin to Historic Ellicott City, Inc. in 1980 in the interest of its preservation. I have five daughters, one of whom is now deceased, five grandchildren and ten great-grandchildren. I was born and raised in Howard County.

Debbie Temple is an employee of Howard County government who contacted the authors when we advertised the oral history project sponsored by Historic Ellicott City, Inc. She encouraged us to interview her grandmother, Mrs. Cross, and contributed many details to the family story:

My great-grandfather's family settled in the town of Daisy, Maryland, in western Howard County, in the mid-1800s, where they worked on many farms in the area, several of which belonged to Edwin Warfield, who was governor of Maryland from 1904 to 1908. Some of the black families

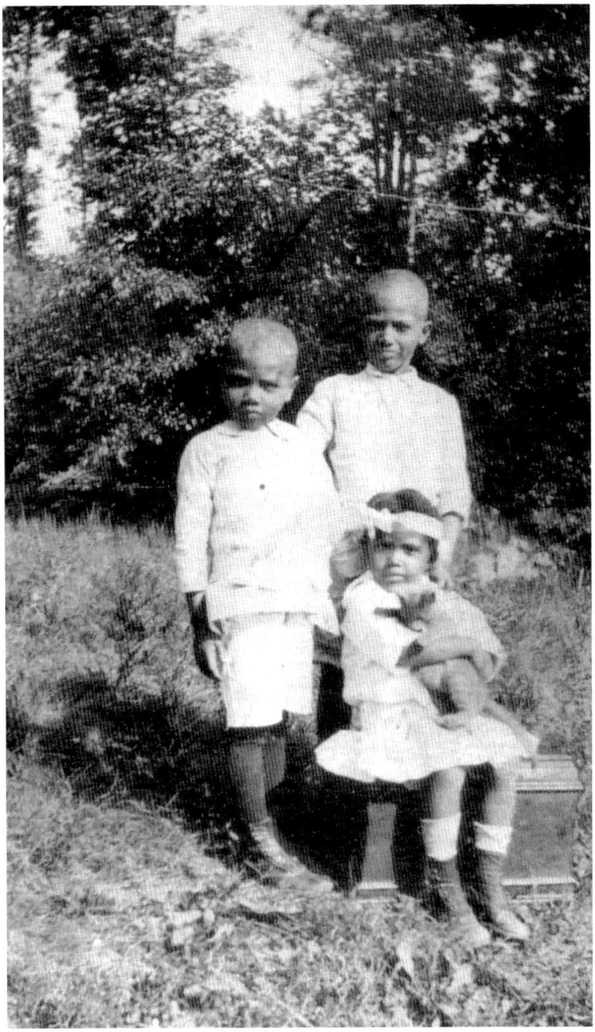

Gladys Stanton and her brothers in the 1920s. *Courtesy of Debbie Temple.*

that settled in and around Daisy had relatives who worked as slaves for the Warfields.

Daisy, Maryland, was founded in 1882, and is southeast of Lisbon, off Route 144, its crossroads existing at Daisy and Union Chapel Roads. My maternal great-grandparents, Fannie Fletcher Stanton and John Henry Stanton, were married in Daisy on October 24, 1910. My grandmother was born in Daisy on February 22, 1915.

My maternal great-grandparents, with their children in tow, moved from Daisy to Ellicott City, where they owned their home and farmed the land, raising hogs, chickens, rabbits, fruit and vegetables, and selling their goods to markets in the area. Imagine having a farm today right within the historic district! The Thomas Isaac Log Cabin, built circa 1780, was originally located alongside my great-grandparents' house on their Merryman Street property in Ellicott City. In 1870, the log cabin served as the mission church of St. Luke African Methodist Episcopal Church in Ellicott City.

In 1980, workers dismantled the building and numbered and marked each stone, log and board, which they stored on county property until the cabin could be reassembled in its new location at Main Street and Ellicott Mills Drive. Historic Ellicott City, Inc. held a groundbreaking ceremony at the new location on April 26, 1985, and transferred ownership of the property to the county in 1988.

My great-grandmother, Fannie Stanton, and my grandmother donated the log cabin to the Howard County Department of Recreation and Parks.

It is the oldest structure on Main Street. On July 16, 1988, the official dedication ceremony of the Thomas Isaac Log Cabin was attended by the Cross/Stanton family; the Howard County executive, Elizabeth Bobo; the Howard County Council; Senator James Clark; and various other members of the community.

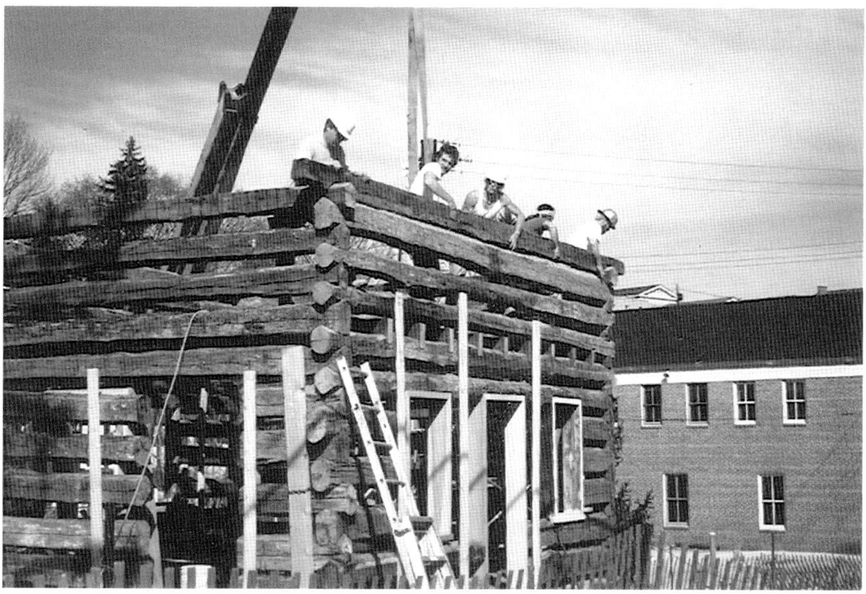

The Thomas Isaac Log Cabin reconstruction. *Courtesy of Historic Ellicott City, Inc.*

The cost to rebuild, which included a Maryland Historic Trust grant of $18,715, was approximately $125,000. The cabin has been used for living history presentations, including "Two Centuries on Main Street."

> *My grandmother was married for fifty-nine years to Ambrose D. Cross, a longtime Howard County legend and proud World War II veteran. At the time of his death, at the age of eighty, on December 13, 1991, he was named in a* Baltimore Sun *article and a* Howard County Times *article as the oldest county employee. He worked for the Howard County Circuit Court as courtroom bailiff. All of the judges and circuit court staffers loved and respected him. In 1989, Bob Turk of WJZ TV honored him with the Channel 13 salute pin in a televised tribute to his dedication, work ethic, gentle kindness, helpfulness and good humor. My grandfather also worked at the Main Street Post Office, retiring in 1975 after forty-three years, as the first of Howard County's black postal workers, at Commercial and Farmer's Bank and at Leidig's Bakery—all on Main Street. In 1992, the Howard County Council, at the behest of Judge Cornelius Sybert and the other circuit court judges, unanimously approved a resolution authorizing the naming of the jury assembly room in the courthouse in honor of my grandfather—the Ambrose D. Cross Jury Assembly Room.*

"I have seen lots of change over the years," Cross remembered.

> *When we moved here, Columbia Pike was a dirt road, and our house was a log cabin, which we have added to over time. The front porch made the house seem closer to the road. I stayed home and looked after the children, and my husband worked at odd jobs to make a decent living. In the early days, he would work in the cornfields for a dollar a day plus his dinner. I remember the grocery stores on Main Street—Yates, Paul's Market, the A&P and the American Store that became the Acme. The lettuce used to come in wooden crates and they would save the crates and sell them to my husband, and he would break them up and sell them for kindling to make some extra money.*
>
> *I also remember Joe Berger's shop from about fifty years ago—I think it was where the Judge's Bench is now. Sometimes I would give the children a few pennies and they would go there and get the penny candy—he would always let them load up bags full. We talked about the log cabin next door to my parents' house on Merryman Street. They raised pigs and chickens and used the cabin to store tools.*

"Born and bred in Ellicott City, from 1957 through 1965, I attended elementary school at St. Paul's Catholic School, which at the time was one of the very few integrated schools in the county," Temple said.

> *It was on St. Paul Street, which is off of Maryland Avenue. My grandfather, Mr. Ambrose Cross, walked me to school every day and we often took the Tiber Alley route. Clark's storage and livery stables were on Tiber Alley. I remember Paul's Market, the Howard House, Miller Chevrolet, Leidig's Bakery, Dee's Kitchen, Votta's Shoe Shop, Caplan's, the 5 & 10 Cent Store, Dr. Benny Mellor's pharmacy, the* Ellicott City Times, *Yates Market, the Ellicott City Cab Company, Acme Supermarket, Clark's Hardware, the Ellicott Movie Theater, Taylor's Furniture Store, gasoline filling stations, all of these and many other businesses within walking distance of each other along Main Street. Although Howard County was considered "country" back then, Ellicott City was a big city, albeit a small big city!*

The Commercial Hub of the County

In the early days, "Ellicott City was a thriving commercial hub centered on the Ellicott's Mill," according to Jean Hannon.

> *The town held feed and grain stores, blacksmiths, grocery stores, etc. When it also became the county seat, additional commerce was created by the lawyers and their clients. During the days when the B&O Railroad ran its passenger service from Mount Claire to Ellicott City, the area also became a summer home for many vacationing Baltimoreans. At one time, both passenger trains and streetcars ran to Ellicott City. As the automobile rose in importance, Ellicott City's commerce dropped. A new highway bypassing the town and new shopping centers close by saw most of the small businesses close. In 1900, there were thirteen grocery stores; in 1975 there were three. Between 1955 and 1965, many empty shops were rented as apartments and the business area suffered a decline.*

A local (unidentified) store ledger that covered the years from 1916 to 1923 paints a picture very different from today's Ellicott City. Spidery handwriting in black fountain pen ink records 425 pages of entries over

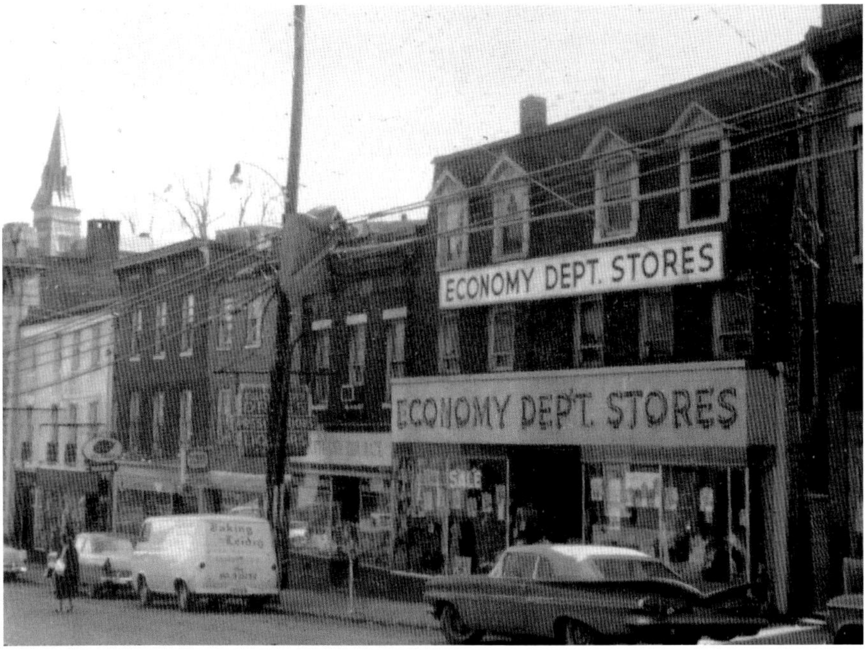

The Economy Store. *Courtesy of Herb Johl.*

that time period, averaging only nine hundred purchases per year. Many very familiar names are listed on these pages of history. In March 1916, the sheriff, Julius Wosch, paid one dollar for a pair of straps. Sheriff Wosch was a legend in the town, often arresting drunks and vagrants and ordering them to report to the jail—and they did, on their own. It seems that everyone needed supplies for their horses, from funeral home operators Hillsinger and Easton to mill proprietors Gambrill, Dickey and Burgess to ex-governor Warfield to Charles Carroll of Home Wood. Purchases included everything from mule bits for twenty-five cents; buckets of grease; and curry combs and martingales (control tack for horses) for ninety cents.

The shop also made a variety of repairs, from replacing suitcase straps to sharpening clippers to refurbishing umbrellas to repairing a mailbag for Rock Hill College. Most purchasers were local; the outsiders were noted as coming from Catonsville, Elkridge and Jessup. In addition to the various Dorseys, Ridgelys and Moxleys represented, Rock Hill College and the Howard Sanitarium also made purchases. The store sold everything from umbrellas to "dandy" brushes, hoof oil to cow tails. "I remember my grandmother telling me that the cow tails were used to swat flies," said Debbie Temple.

INTERVIEW WITH JEAN KEENAN

"In 1934, when I was in the third grade, my family moved to Ellicott City from Catonsville," said Jean Keenan.

> *We lived here until 1941, when we moved back to Catonsville. I went to the Ellicott City High School when it was located on College Avenue, where condominiums are now. The building housed the first through eleventh grades—there was no kindergarten and no twelfth grade. I still visit my seventh-grade teacher, Miss Wilhelmina Oldfield, who is now ninety-five and still lives in Ellicott City. They had a big graduation ceremony at the end of seventh grade, as some of the boys lived on farms and that would be the end of their education as they were needed to help on the farm. The school had a big wooden gym with a big stage. It was a community room and they put on shows. I remember* Happy Johnny*—a musical comedy—and a talent show. Dapper Dan played the fiddle while sitting on it.*
>
> *We lived on Columbia Road, opposite Hunt Avenue. My parents bought the house from the Meyers family. I had to walk to school, and there were no*

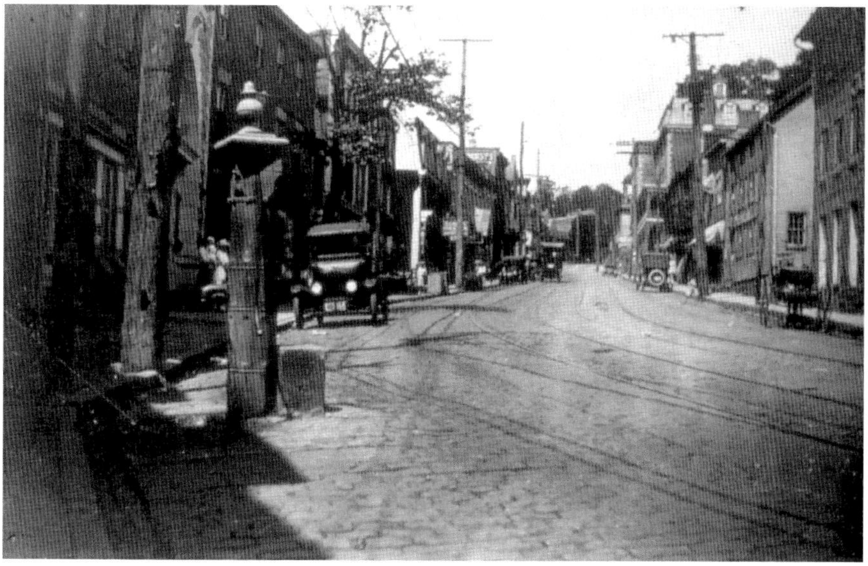

Main Street with utility poles and the Oldfield water pump. *Courtesy of Herb Johl.*

sidewalks. My mother was very worried about my safety and fussed with the school board. It didn't make any sense—the bus rode right past us—so eventually they let it pick us up. I loved going to school there. In 1939, they opened a new high school on Montgomery Road, where there is a middle school now. I was in the first freshman class in the new school and went there for two years before we moved back to Catonsville.

Before World War II, Ellicott City was a great little town. It was the only place where you could buy anything, unless you went to Baltimore. We bought our groceries from Yates Market. We only had one car, and it was gone all day since my father took it to work, so we would call Yates and put in our order and they would deliver it to us. My father worked on Main Street, first at Peddicord's Appliance Store and later at Prudential Insurance.

There were a lot of stores. Caplan's had everything—shoes, clothes. I wore long cotton hose, rolled. One time my mother gave me the money to buy a new pair of hose and Mrs. Caplan asked me what color I wanted—light, dark? I told her I wanted a color that didn't show dirt very much! Rosenstock's was a popular place too, but it was more for the farmers, selling overalls and boots. I went to Taylor's to buy violin strings. I took a class in violin, offered through school, on the second or third floor of the IOOF [Independent Order of Odd Fellows] *building on Main Street.*

I took piano lessons in Catonsville and rode the streetcar to get there. I would ride to the Catonsville Junction and transfer. There was a big hill we had to ride, and the straps would swing and we would sway—I really dreaded that part of the ride. We also took the streetcar to Baltimore to shop for clothes. The street in Ellicott City was very narrow—it still is—and with parking on both sides and two sets of tracks sometimes it was too little space for the streetcar to get through—sometimes a car blocked the way. The conductor would start clanking his bell until someone came and moved the car. The conductors also liked to stop partway down the street and go for coffee. One time when the conductor went for coffee the car kept going, but no one was hurt.

Ben Mellor ran a drugstore with a soda fountain. The Economy Department Store had a little of everything—clothes, women's stuff. They had a window display filled with high-heeled shoes—the heels must have been four inches high—and we liked to look at them. There was a ladies' dress shop and two banks, Patapsco National and Farmers and Mechanics. I remember Mary Betts and her husband—one worked in each bank. Elmer Cavey was in charge of Commercial and Farmers.

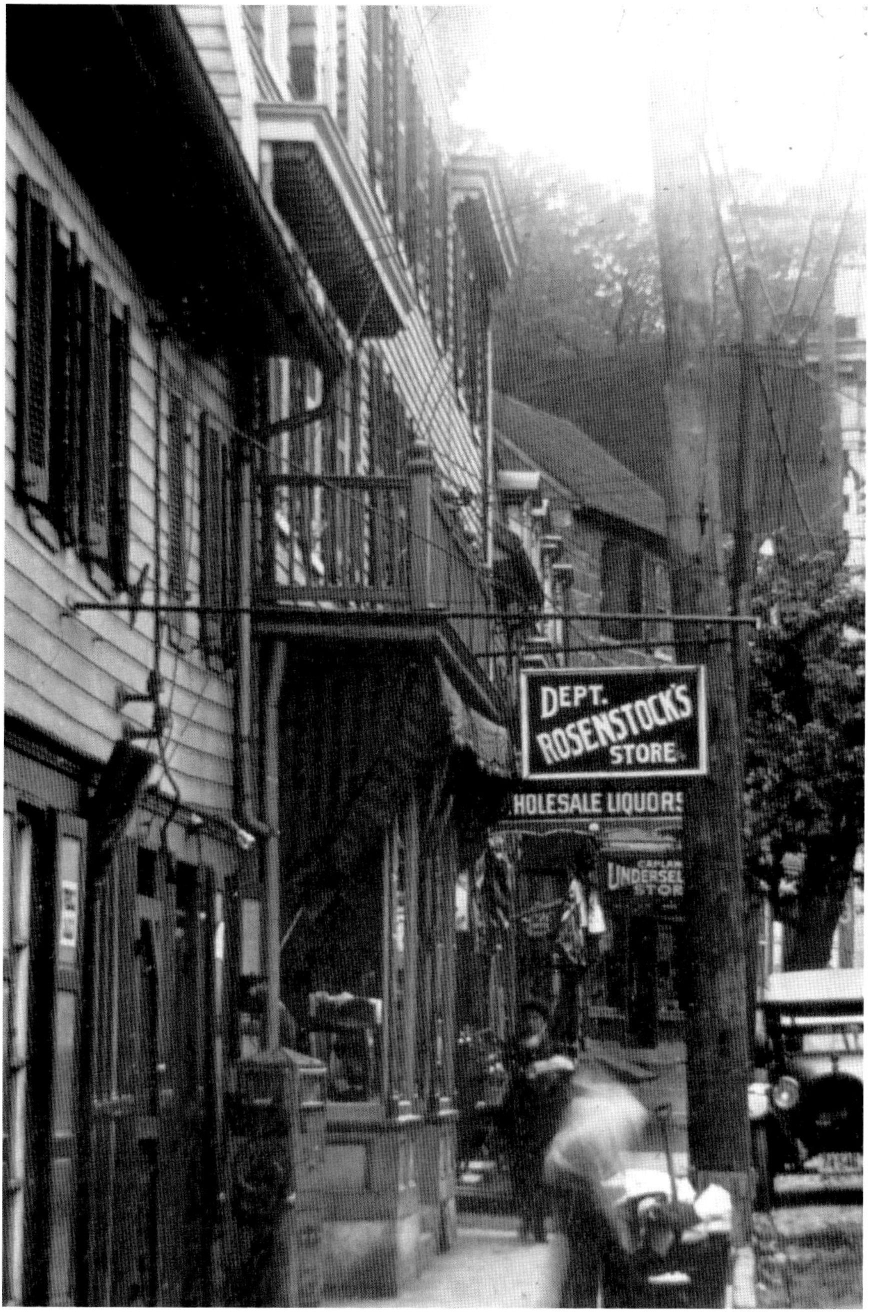

Rosenstock's Department Store. *Courtesy of Herb John.*

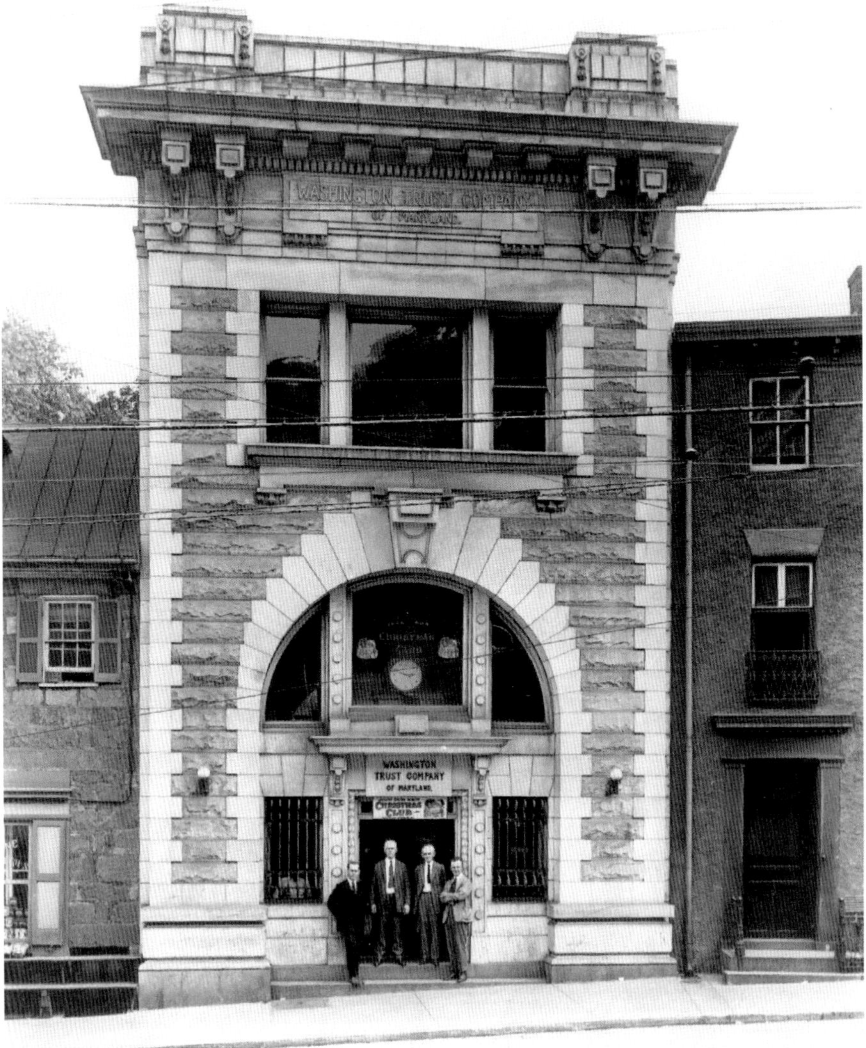

Washington Trust Bank; note the Christmas Club sign in the window. *Courtesy of Victoria Goeller.*

In the 1930s, the county's Health Department Clinic was located in the building where Tersiguel's is now. There was one doctor—Dr. Shrop—and two nurses—Margaret Noel and Marguerite Lauper—for the whole county. Every summer the nurses would do a "summer roundup," and my mother rode with them to help out. They would visit every home with school-age children in the county and make sure they had the shots they needed before school.

In the summertime, we had to make our own fun. I played lots of Monopoly. There was a chicken house right over the hill from our house. I couldn't eat chicken while we raised them because they were like pets. Once we got rid of the chickens, my mother painted the chicken house and made it into a play house for us. We could play dolls in there and even have sleepovers. Another thing I liked to do was decorate shoe boxes with pictures of draperies and things I'd cut out of catalogues. Movie magazines were popular then, and I'd make scrapbooks out of pictures of the movie stars. At night we'd listen to the Lux Radio Theatre, Kate Smith *and mystery shows like* The Shadow *and* Dick Tracy *on the radio. Sometimes on the weekend we'd sit out in front of our house on Columbia Pike and count cars—there were never more than one hundred cars all day—counting both ways—and they were all Buicks or Chevys.*

We went to the Presbyterian church that is now the home of the Howard County Historical Society. William Collier was the supervisor of the summer school. He would go to Florida every winter and bring back crates of oranges. At Christmas we would get net stockings filled with candy and an orange. A group of young people from the church used to visit the jail. We'd sit around a big table and have dinner with the prisoners. I don't think there were any murderers there or anything else that serious—but I was scared, but I did it. Marshall Page was the minister. He knew a lot about Maryland history and had a regular fifteen-minute show about it on WBAL radio. He would take a few kids with him when he did the show. I would play "Maryland My Maryland" on the piano and other kids would read ads for local places like Mellor's and Caplan's.

I had a pretty good voice and my mother got me to try out for a show called Uncle Jack's Kiddie Club, *which was on the radio on Saturday mornings from the Hippodrome Theatre in Baltimore. I sang on the show a couple of times.*

Roger Carter's Memories

The Roger Carter Recreation Center was named for Roger Sylvester Carter, an African American community leader and business owner. Born in Guilford, Maryland, in 1916 to Samuel and Elizabeth (Kelly) Carter, he continued a family tradition of business ownership. In the 1940s, Carter opened a garage and auto mechanics shop in Ellicott City at Rogers Avenue and Frederick Road, next to the site of the Ellicott City Colored School. In 1948, he began providing bus transportation for African American students around the county. As county schools were integrated, he provided bus service for students of all races. In 1977, Historic Ellicott City, Inc. invited local community members to share their memories of Main Street. President Herb Johl recorded the recollections, including this by Roger Carter:

> *I have played Santa Claus quite a number of times and quite a lot of funny things have happened. I've been involved in Head Start every year since it's been here. I've got children now that I hauled when they were three years old going to Head Start and now they're going to high school in the senior class, and it's really amazing to see those little kids and follow them up to where they're graduating this year. Some of the experiences that I had playing Santa Claus were with the Head Start, and there's one experience that I'll never forget. One Christmas we had a school in Guilford, one in Ellicott City, one in Atholton and one in Cooksville, and I had to play Santa Claus to all four schools the same day.*
>
> *I had started at Guilford and had got to Ellicott City and was going out Route 40 all dressed up like Santa Claus and flying, and a state police stopped me. And when he stopped and pulled me over he said, "You ought to have reindeer instead of a bus! Where are you going?" I said, "Officer, Sir, I know I'm speeding but I've got to be at Lisbon for the little Head Start children." He said, "Well, I tell you what. This is going to be one time that Santa Claus is going to get an escort." He escorted me straight to Lisbon school, came in and told the people what he had done to Santa Claus. That in itself is an experience that I have never forgotten—to be dressed as Santa Claus and be escorted to the school.*
>
> *And then some other experiences I've had, just last year—by the way, this Friday night I'll be Santa Claus at Guilford for the Head Start program; I've been Santa year after year, just a ritual—last year we had a program*

at Glenmar and I played Santa Claus. I had been driving the bus and all the kids knew my voice. They could tell me a mile away. I dressed up, and this particular outfit had nothing to cover your face; I'll fix 'em. I went on anyway and this was the first time they had seen Santa Claus with dark glasses on. I bought all the kids a book with picture stories in them. So here I am the next morning driving the bus up the road, and they say, "Oh, Mr. Carter! Santa Claus was there last night and here's a present he gave us. He's the nicest Santa Claus we ever met." And I'm sitting there trying to keep from laughing. It has really done something to me to be able to work with other people's children. I love children and it's always been my weakness. I guess it always will be and I know Friday coming will be just another time that I'll be happy that I can make some kids happy.

Roger Carter received many awards for his service to the community. They include the Youth Award from the Greater Baltimore YMCA and a Head Start Service Award. In 1978, he was honored as the Civic Leader of the Year by the Greater Howard County Chamber of Commerce and presented with the Business Community Award by the Alliance Toward an Active Community. Highly respected in the community, he was the first African American man invited to join the Ellicott City Rotary. Roger Carter was beloved by generations of Howard County schoolchildren and their parents for his generosity and caring. He died in 1982, and the funeral procession extended for over a mile. On August 9, 1984, the Ellicott City Neighborhood Center was renamed for him.

Interview with Sylvia Sheppard and Norma Caloyianis

The Ellicott City High School was on Park Avenue from 1902 until 1925. It relocated to College Avenue in 1925. Next, the school moved to Montgomery Road in 1939, with the first graduating class that attended classes there for all four years graduating in 1943. In 1923, when the school was on Park Avenue, the students published a monthly newspaper called the *Focus*. That year James Clark, who went on to be president of the Maryland Senate, was one of the "Class News" editors. The students believed that "every first class high school boasts a paper…ECHS is a first class high school and, therefore, we must have a paper." An amazing article in the October issue of the paper announced the creation of an office. It's hard to imagine a school without one today, but apparently it was noteworthy in 1923:

> *A large desk, on which may be found piles and piles of papers—absentee lists, delinquent lists, book reports, daily reports, etc.—constitutes the main furniture. Last year, these piles and piles of papers would have been scattered about almost anywhere…Since we have become acquainted with the office we do not see how we could do without it. It is a necessity. The keys of each room in the high school department would probably be lost if they did not have a place here.*

In addition to class reports and a few short stories, the paper included a few jokes, like:

> *The teacher told the class to write a theme on "What would I do if I had a million dollars." At the end of the period, Wilson Hood had not written a word.*
>
> *"Wilson, where is your theme?" asked the teacher.*
>
> *"There," he said, "That's what I would do if I had a million dollars—Nothing."*

Sylvia Cavey Sheppard and Nora Valmas Caloyianis have known each other since first grade and were in the first graduating class of the Ellicott City High School on Montgomery Road in 1943—there were forty-three students in that class. Because of the war and the paper shortage they had no yearbook.

"One of the best days was Rally Day," said Sheppard.

> *We would compete in sports with students from Elkridge, West Friendship and Clarksville. The principal was John Yingling. He was a stern taskmaster. He would make us do a half hour of calisthenics outside every day before school started. If the weather was really bad, we would exercise in the gym. A few years ago, there was a class reunion at the Crab Shanty Restaurant, and one of our teachers, Wilhelmina Oldfield, attended at age ninety-one.*
>
> *I was born in 1926. My father owned Cavey Brothers Barbershop on Main Street for over sixty years—1926 to 1994. It was originally Babylon's Barbershop. It was in three locations, including where the Rosenstock building was and later where Stillridge Herb Farm was. Until*

I was about six years old, we lived in a house abutting the railroad tracks. Then we moved to Gray's farm. My grandfather worked as a gandy dancer [a railroad laborer] *for the B&O Railroad. When we lived on the farm, we would go by boat to Ellicott City, along River Road. Once, when I was very young, I had a special angora suit. My mother saw me in the boat and got upset, thinking that if the suit got wet it would be ruined.*

Caloyianis's father, John Valmas, and her uncle, his brother Paul, owned Valmas Bros. Restaurant. It was where the Phoenix Emporium is now. Before that, the restaurant was called the Maryland Restaurant.

"Around 1952, the restaurant moved to where Jordan's Restaurant is now [on the south side of lower Main Street]," said Caloyianis. "They were in business from 1926 to 1973, closing after the flood caused by Tropical Storm Agnes. In the first store, one side was the restaurant and the other side had homemade candies. At Easter time, we had someone in to personalize and decorate the candy." Caloyianis and Sheppard both especially remembered the panorama sugar eggs with the scenes inside.

On Friday and Saturday nights, the farmers would come to town to eat at Valmas Bros. Restaurant and get their hair cut at Cavey's Barbershop. "It was nice growing up when we did—there was no crime," said Caloyianis.

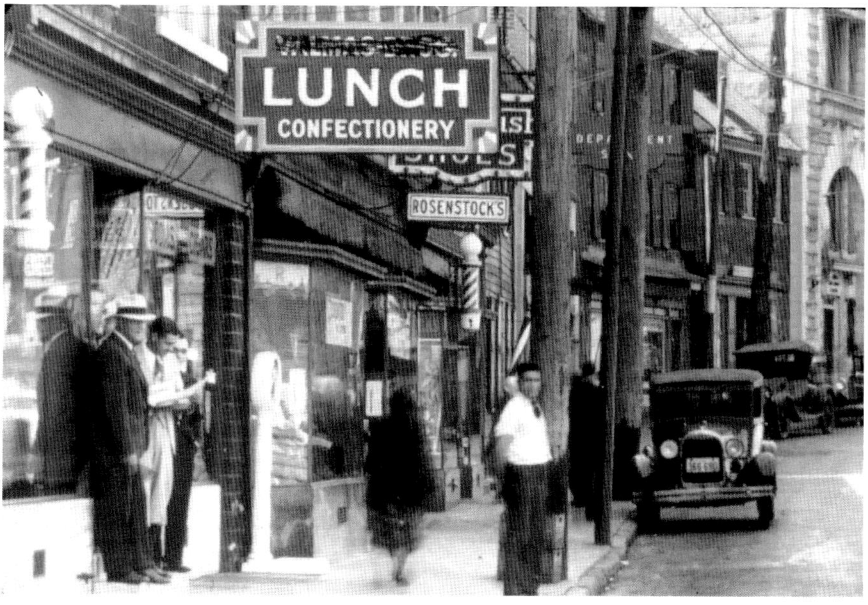

Valmas Bros. Restaurant. *Courtesy of Herb Johl.*

"No one locked their doors. Julius Wosch was chief of police and he lived on Main Street. One of the worst crimes around at the time was getting drunk. Wosch would send the drunks up to the jail—and they knew they had to go and went without being taken. A store called McDonald's was where the Trolley Stop is now. That was where you bought trolley tickets and penny candy. Later the place became what we called 'The Bloody Bucket.'"

"I remember 'Hood's Store' in the 1930s and '40s, directly across the street from the Opera House," Sheppard said.

> *It was a general store that had everything—food, magazines, barrels of pickles and hard candy. I remember Delp's Cab Company and Shaw's, next door to Hood's. I remember Mal Easton of Easton's Funeral Home on Main Street. He could cure warts by waving a knotted string over the affected area. The wart would go away.*
>
> *During the Depression, when hobos would rap on the door and ask for a sandwich, my mother always fixed them something. We finished school in eleven years instead of the usual twelve (there was no eighth grade), which made us too young to work in many places. I worked for a year at the Continental Mill and then got a job in Baltimore. I took the train to Camden station, then a streetcar to my job at Charles and Chase Streets.*

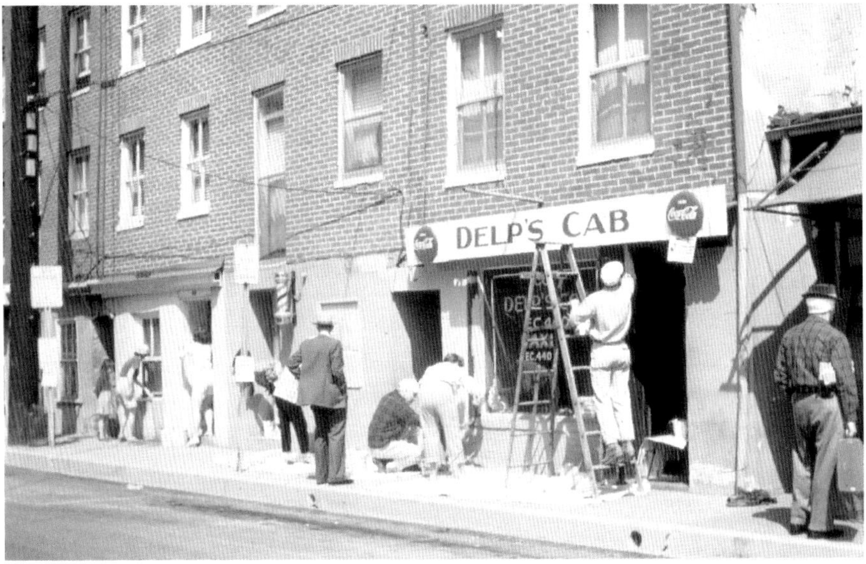

Delp's Cab Company. *Courtesy of Herb Johl.*

> *It was fun. Since I rode every day, if I was a few minutes late or they were a few minutes early, they would blow the horn and wait for me. I met people from Sykesville that I wouldn't have met otherwise, riding the train. I bought a book of tickets, but don't remember the cost.*

Sheppard also remembered roller skating down the sidewalk on Main Street: "We never got seriously hurt but we had our share of skinned knees. We also liked to sit on waxed paper and slide down 'the Rock.'"

"The Rock" is a large outcropping of granite on the north side of Main Street between Ellicott's Country Store and the law offices of Fishbein and Fishbein, which incorporates part of the rock in its foundation. This three-story slab of granite is awesome. For many years, the site was presentable but not noteworthy, attracting weeds, trash and graffiti. Frank DiPietro, one of the owners of Main Street's Mumbles & Squeaks Toy Shoppe, cleaned it up and planted it with flowers as part of the garden celebration of 225 years of Ellicott City history in 1997, and it won a first-place award in its category.

Interview with Ed Lilley

"My father's parents settled in Oella," Ed Lilley said.

> *My grandfather was a motorman for the streetcars. My grandfather died when my father was ten, in the 1920s. He was laid out in the living room of their house on a marble slab. Following the burial, the horse drawing the hearse got spooked at the cemetery and ran off down the hill. As a child, my father used to swim in the Patapsco River, north of the bridge. When the Dickey* [textile] *Mill would get ready to dump the dye they were using into the river, a whistle would warn the kids to get out of the river before the dye got to them. My father, who had lost the use of a leg due to illness as a child, worked at the Doughnut Corporation as a secretary for the plant manager during World War II. He got to know a lot of the millworkers and corresponded with them when they left to serve in the war. Around that time, my mother worked at the shirt factory on Fels Lane with Doris Thompson. I remember my family shopping at the Acme here, as well as at the Patapsco Pharmacy. My father had an insurance agency on Main Street for many years, and I joined the business after graduating from college in the late 1960s. After we closed the insurance business, I opened up the Christmas Company in the same location. I had always loved Christmas and many*

places I visited had stores with Christmas ornaments, so I thought that would be a good idea for Ellicott City as well.

The shop, now closed, was well known for its impressive wall of Christmas ornaments, as well as for frequent visits from German nutcracker makers.

The Ellicott City Volunteer Firemen's Carnival: Interview with Jean Keenan

To aid in fundraising for equipment, maintenance and operating expenses, the first Volunteer Firemen's Carnival was held from September 3 to 6, 1924, at the B&O Railroad Depot Yard on Maryland Avenue. Souvenir programs included a photograph of the members of Engine and Hose No. 1 and proclaimed "Service—Anywhere—Anytime." The carnival was a success, raising $2,500.

In 1934, the eleventh annual carnival hosted a public wedding. Rachel Yingling of Ellicott City, age seventeen, and James Hobbs III of West Friendship, age eighteen and fresh from military service, were married amid a sea of well-wishers. Janet Kusterer met the couple several years ago, and they shared some details of the event. Arrangements were made by Mrs. G. Ray Helm. Hutzler's provided the wedding gown and veil, S&N Katz the ring and Charles H. Cook & Son the flowers. Yingling's mother made the bridesmaids' dresses, in shades of blue, pink, purple and yellow. Local merchants showered the couple with gifts. The wedding had been widely advertised, and the bridal couple got caught in the snarled traffic on their way to the wedding. The ceremony took place on an elevated pavilion, and all carnival activity ceased for that time. People actually climbed trees and stood on cars to see it. The day after the wedding, the couple returned to the carnival.

By 1959, interest in the annual carnivals was waning, and the event was discontinued. A fire tax was levied to defray the department's operating expenses and continues to this day.

Nora Valmas Caloyianis remembered the carnival:

It was a "big thing" and involved a big parade and people from miles around. It was a fundraiser for the volunteer fire department. My father, John Valmas, was a volunteer fireman. I remember the fire truck stopping in front of the restaurant to pick up my father on the way to a fire, and he would get on still wearing his apron. I also remember him working with other men to move cars out of the path of the trolley, rocking them back and forth to move them.

"When growing up as a kid near Ellicott City in the late '30s and early '40s, one of the things I really looked forward to in those l-o-n-n-g days of summer was the Volunteer Fire Department Carnival," said Jean Keenan.

This great event was held from the very last Friday of July into the first week of August. The carnival always began on a Friday and a tremendous parade was held late the next afternoon.

The parade formed at the corner of Rogers Avenue and Main Street and wound down through the town and up College Avenue to the playground of the Ellicott City School. At that time, the school housed the first through eleventh grades. The playground now is covered with condos and the school has also been converted to condos.

Being a firemen's parade, there were engines, ambulances and rescue squads representing many communities in Howard and surrounding counties. Prizes were awarded for the best appearing representatives and, I believe, to the company that came the longest distance. Their sirens would blast out—sometimes more than one at a time—with a deafening but thrilling sound to us kids.

Our family was most fortunate that we were invited to sit on the porch of the double house owned by Mary and Norman Betts next to Talbott's Lumber Company, which today is the Ellicott Mills Brewing Company. From that vantage point, we could really see. The Queen of the Carnival riding on the back of a convertible, all kinds of clowns, several bands, parading political figures, the little Austin car which seemed to regurgitate at least a dozen clowns, the crazy car which "reared up" on its back axle and turned round and round, the Ladies' Auxiliary of the Fire Department, the decorated bicycles and the man on stilts were some parade entries that I looked forward to seeing in the parade every year.

In several years, there were actual weddings performed. On at least one occasion, the bridal party nearly missed the wedding because of all the traffic in Ellicott City. Often stars from the vaudeville show at the Hippodrome Theatre in Baltimore were brought out from town to sing or dance. Other favorites were a talent show and a jitterbug contest, as well as square dancing and roller skating exhibitions, jugglers and fire-eaters. Remember, these were days prior to television so seeing these acts was a real *treat, especially to people living in the country (as Ellicott City and Howard County were then).*

Of course, the reason for holding the carnival was to raise money for the strictly volunteer fire department. They did not receive money for their work in fighting fires and manning the ambulance. Therefore there were many opportunities at the carnival to spend our saved-up nickels and dimes.

One such opportunity was the penny pitch, trying to toss a penny into a floating saucer. The older boys and men tried to boast of their muscle power by pounding a lever that would send a metal disc up a tower and ring a gong. There were also balloon darts and wheels to try to win stuffed animals. Always there was the popular bingo tent with prizes, which were usually household items and carnival glass. In 1934, fifty sets of dishes were chanced off one night.

Not to be left out were the booths with all kinds of foods from a cold plate supper for fifty-five cents to ice cream and hot dogs and hamburgers. Of course there were cotton candy and soft drinks, too. A variety of booths were erected with wheels where folks could win such things as hams, blankets or ten pounds of sugar if they were lucky. In 1941, when I was fourteen, there was a booth offering nothing but umbrellas! I played number fourteen and won! That didn't happen very often.

The one favorite attraction that I remember was the stuntman who climbed a ladder about twenty-five to thirty feet into the air and jumped into a big pool, similar to the above-ground pools of today. This was a crowd-holder since it did not happen until the carnival was nearly over each night. There would be a drumroll and spotlight as the daredevil climbed the ladder. Then there would be dead silence until he made the plunge into the pool, followed by great applause.

Each year a new car would be chanced off. For many years, this was a Chevrolet supplied by the Miller Chevrolet Company. In other years, it would be a Ford or a Plymouth. The firemen would start weeks in advance and drive the car to places such as Glen Burnie, Catonsville or the Enchanted Forest, where there were lots of people to buy chances. The grand drawing was always held on the very last night of the carnival.

The carnivals continued until 1959, except for a hiatus during the years of World War II. After the war, the location was moved to the grounds of the new Ellicott City High School, which opened in 1939 on Montgomery Road. Today this is the Ellicott Mills Middle School. Times have changed greatly, but my memories are still vivid. Oh, how I long to spend just one more evening at the carnival.

SHOPPING TRIPS TO THE SMALL "BIG CITY": INTERVIEWS WITH JAMES ROBEY AND CHARLOTTE HOLLAND

"I was born and raised in the mill town of Daniels, near Ellicott City in Baltimore County," said James Robey.

> *My father was an electrician at the mill and my mother was a stay-at-home housewife. I worked in the mill at Daniels before I joined the police department. You had to work at the mill to live in Daniels, so after our first child was born in 1963 and I didn't want to work in the mill anymore, we moved to a trailer park in Woodstock. We later moved to Baltimore County for a while and then moved to Ellicott City, near Route 40, in 1987.*
>
> *My earliest memory of Ellicott City was going there to shop. This was in the late 1940s, early '50s. We bought clothes, went to Cavey's Barbershop for haircuts and got our furniture from Taylor's. In the late 1950s, I went to Howard High School. After school I would hitch a ride to Ellicott City and then meet the mailman. I'd give him twenty-five cents to let me ride home with him in the mail truck. On Saturdays, we would go to Eddie's Drugstore next to the movies and go to the movies and watch westerns and eat popcorn. We shopped at Yates Market, too.*

"My family moved to my father's family farm in August 1947," recalled Charlotte Holland.

> *We lived there for six years, and during that time Ellicott City was our Saturday shopping place. For us kids it was an atmosphere of excitement. We lived on a farm. The small village of Lisbon was our local metropolis and it was tiny. Coming into Ellicott City meant access to things we didn't have in a farm community. There were six children in my family and I was the youngest. If the kids wanted to come, that was what we did, and it was a day we could buy things. I remember big excitement for us was looking for the newest cowboy magazines. Mom would pick up groceries—at Yates or Paul's.*
>
> *I remember one particular visit when my great-uncle Nick came with us and that's when I first saw the railroad station. We went up to the*

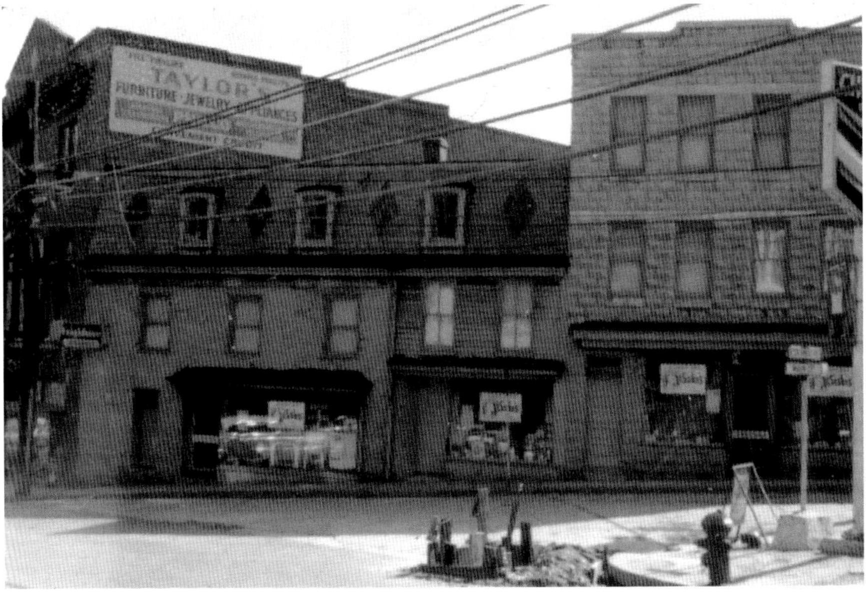

Taylor's Department Store. *Courtesy of Herb Johl.*

station and it really was a kind of a pretty barren and dirty place as I remember it, but I thought it was so exciting because Uncle Nick had been out west. His mother had a brother who had a store out in what is now Kansas City. She would send the children out there for visits. Uncle Nick went out and forgot to come back, and he just kept traveling. He took the train as far west as Ohio, then traveled by stagecoach. I think he came back in his sixties. He told me how the Ellicott City railroad station is the oldest in the country.

I also remember streetcar tracks. My father told me about how the streetcars went to Baltimore. When he was a young man growing up in Lisbon, he knew he'd have to go somewhere else to earn a living. When he was nineteen, somebody drove him into Ellicott City in a wagon and from there he got a streetcar in to Baltimore. He lived in the YMCA and worked as a secretary.

World War II: Interviews with Bill Heber, Russell Ridgely, Al Corun and Travis Harry

"I was born in March 1927 and lived with my grandparents at their farm located where Glenmar Church is now," said Bill Heber.

> *I attended Howard County High School and graduated in 1944. My class had a yearbook. It was a folder with a blue cardboard cover and listed the graduates' names but had no pictures. I joined the Maryland Militia in my junior year of high school. In the militia, I was issued one khaki shirt and pair of pants and had to supply my own boots, guns and field equipment. I did guard duty. We marched in parades for all the holidays, like Fourth of July and Labor Day. Otherwise, I came to Main Street once a month for a haircut. My aunt and uncle used to come visit from Tacoma Park, Maryland, and would give money to us kids to go to the movies on Main Street. That was a rare treat, but for twenty-five cents we saw two movies, some serials and previews. When I came out of the movies on December 7, 1941, I learned about Pearl Harbor. I enlisted in the navy after high school graduation in 1944. After the war, I worked in the Doughnut Corporation machine shop. I remember coming to town occasionally to look at the trains. One time, coal cars crashed and people walked along the track picking up the coal.*
>
> *I remember five- and twenty-five-cent slot machines at Valmas's and Caplan's, Blank's clothing store, on the same side of the street as Caplan's, and the Rosenstock Department Store. There was Peddicord's Appliances, and Clark's Hardware was a mainstay and Yates in three locations—lower Main Street, at Old Columbia Pike and its current location.*

Russell Ridgely and Albert Corun have known each other since they met in Miss Irving's class in third grade. "I was born at 92 Frederick Road [Oella] in an area called Hog Alley in 1927," said Corun. "I had five sisters and two brothers and I was the youngest." Ridgely added, "I lived on Hill Street for four years, age eleven to fourteen. I lived in Ellicott City from 1938 to 1945. I attended Ellicott City Elementary School for two years when it was on College Avenue, and high school on Montgomery Road. The high school is gone now."

"When I was a kid, my father was a bartender in the Columbia Café, which was in what is now Ellicott's Country Store," said Corun. "The bar

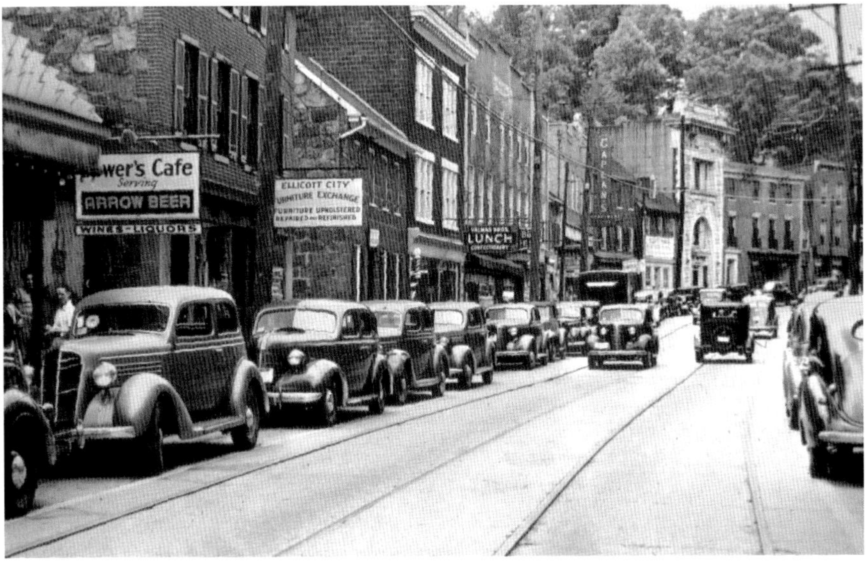

Main Street, 1930s. *Courtesy of Herb Johl.*

had a dirt floor, and in a corner of the bar were rabbits and chickens. People would play cards there and drink liquor. My mother sent me up to get my father one day, but my father made me leave because kids didn't belong there. In the 1930s, I used to swim in the [Patapsco] river."

Corun and Ridgely remembered a fire at the doughnut factory in 1941 and an African American barbershop in the now open space next to the Fishbein and Fishbein law offices. They remembered Mr. Wheatley at the Earl Theatre, which was located where Tiber Park is now, and a pool hall, Valmas's restaurant and Kraft's meat market, which was in the building now housing the Source. They remembered Jake Tasker at the Esso Station and Jimmy Brown at Sorles Market, which became Paul's Market.

Ridgely said, "When I was a kid, I used to cut the lawn of the local dentist, Dr. Brown. The Forget-Me-Not Factory used to be a grocery store. The 'Stoney Lonesome' was the old jail on Emory Street. There were two funeral homes—Easton and Higginbotham."

"I was at Iwo Jima on my eighteenth birthday, February 19, 1945," said Corun. "When the famous flag was raised on February 23, 1945, I had tears in my eyes when I saw it. When I came back from the war, I first worked as a body and fender man for Miller Chevrolet on Main Street. In 1960, I joined the postal department, where I worked for thirty-four years. I remember deep snows and heavy rains in the 1950s and that the building that now houses Tersiguel's then housed the Health Department."

"I remember the covered bridge over the Patapsco and using magnets to collect beer caps," said Ridgely.

> *In 1942–43, the State Guard guarded the railroad bridge. They had rifles but no ammunition. We had various war drives, collecting things like rubber and paper. Drives were led by organizations like the Red Cross or the Boy Scouts. In the guard, we had to go to Camp Meade for two weeks every year. There was rationing—gas, food, shoes, butter, meat, tires. We had stamps to buy gas and groceries. Coins were made of hard cardboard because metal was at a premium. Everyone had victory gardens.*

A few years ago, the Ellicott City B&O Railroad Station Museum sponsored a World War II reenacting program, complete with jeeps on the plaza and a victory garden by the front door.

Ridgely joined the Army Air Force ACERS (Air Corps Enlisted Reserve) in 1944. He was in the Twenty-ninth Division of the Guard. He said, "Charles Miller used to use German POWs to work on his farm. They would be brought to Hardman's Tourist Home at St. John's Lane and Frederick Road

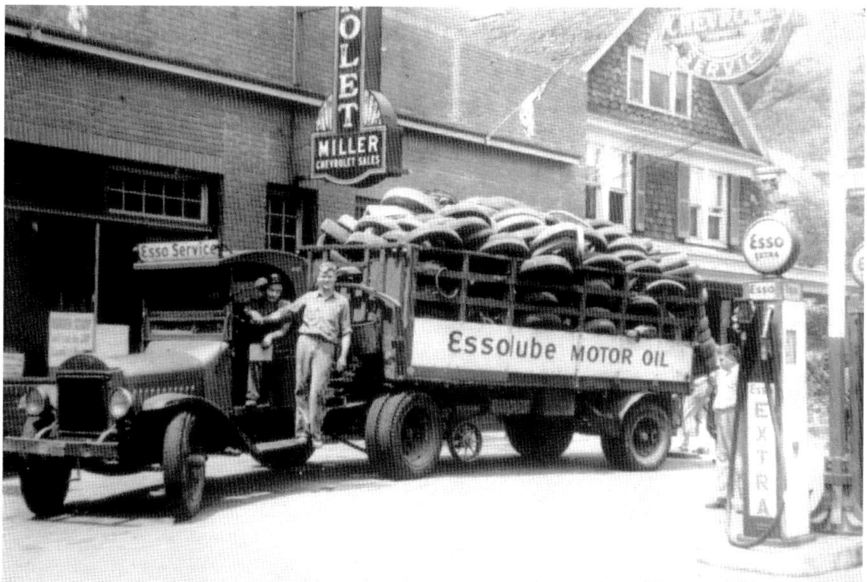

A World War II tire collection. *Courtesy of Herb Johl.*

[west of the historic district]. The POWs stayed at Fort Meade. They usually wore olive-colored overalls and a short-billed cap."

"My grandfather worked for the B&O and brought out flour for the Doughnut Corporation to use in their baking," said Travis Harry.

> *When I was working at a World War II POW reenacting event at the Ellicott City Railroad Station Museum a few years ago, a lady came in and asked if we knew about the victory stone in the Patapsco River. She said her grandfather, who grew up in Catonsville, told her about it. She took us over to where we could see it—it's a red, white and blue "V for Victory" stone painted on a rock by the side of the river. You can see it when the leaves are off the trees from the Baltimore County side of Frederick Road.*

Chapter 5

PAINT AND POLISH

INTERVIEW WITH JEAN HANNON

Jean Hannon was one of the early leaders of the rebirth of Ellicott City:

> *We had a project in 1961 called "PEC"—Paint Ellicott City. I was a member of the Cross Country Garden Club. Around 1960, Sears advertised a beautification contest. The members of the garden club thought that Main Street could use "spiffing up." This was a time when the move was being made to the suburbs, and people were losing interest in the town. Normandy Shopping Center began around then, and businesses were moving out of Main Street and into malls. On Main Street, storefronts were empty.*
>
> *We got the idea of painting the buildings on Main Street from a magazine article in the late '50s about a town called Tiburon, California, which to us looked a lot like Ellicott City. We decided to fix up the area of Main Street from E.T. Clark's* [8000 Main Street] *to Columbia Pike—that was where we thought the nicest buildings were. We were gals sitting around talking, and knowing no limits! We wanted to paint the fronts of all the buildings, and bring in some color. A lot of them were brown with green trim and we didn't like that. We wanted the street to look more interesting. We knew we needed an artist and an architect to help us. I got a Polaroid camera and took pictures of every building, then drew the buildings to scale. The artist and the architect chose the colors we would use, and we took their drawings to show different civic and service organizations.*

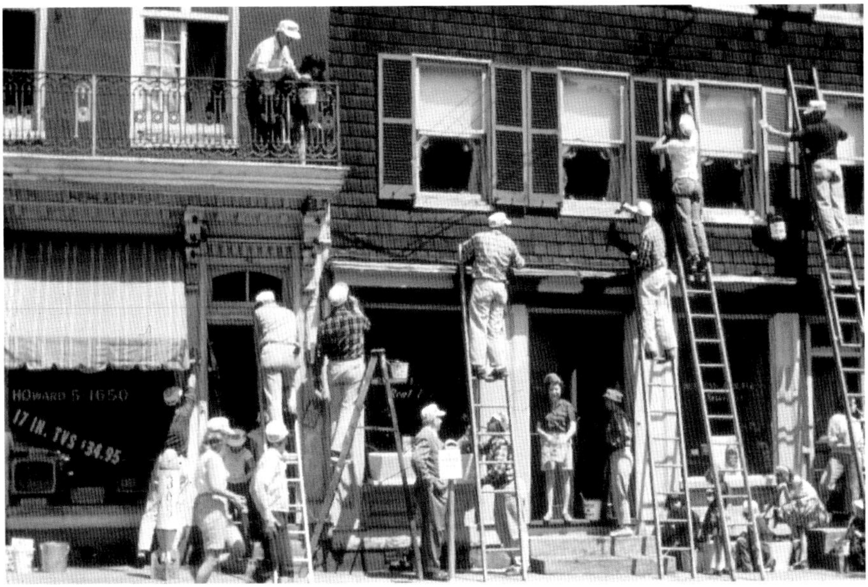

The "Paint Ellicott City" event. *Courtesy of Herb Johl.*

We went to groups like the Rotary and asked for money. The Rotary gave us $1,000, which floored me—I was expecting more like $5. The Split Rail Garden Club joined the project and decided to take over the planting areas on Main Street. We did the façades. The Davis Paint Company donated the paint, and the days we painted [May 20 and 21, 1961], *they came to town with their truck filled with paint, brushes and ladders. A few people on the street painted their buildings themselves but most let us do it.* [Only three buildings from the Patapsco River to Columbia Road remained unpainted. Donations came from everywhere, including thirty dozen doughnuts from the Doughnut Corporation of America, just on the other side of the Patapsco River.]

We called it "Operation Face Lift." The building that later was the Margaret Smith Gallery had a red, white and blue mailbox in front of it, so we painted the building red, white and blue as well. The building next door was gray and yellow. It took months of planning and lots of people. That day the high school band played for us on the Railroad Plaza. The high school shop class made window boxes for the buildings. We had high school students babysitting the young kids. It was a big deal.

The town was overpopulated with signs. Coca-Cola signs were everywhere. That was also a year for the House and Garden tour. That year they and Sears gave a prize for the most important community contribution by a garden club. We won $1,000. Frances Mason and I went to collect the prize and tried to decide what to do with it. Frances thought we should use it to open an antiques shop. Dr. Fitz gave us the building to use and didn't charge us any rent. Ian Crawford and Ada McCallum, the architects who helped us with the painting, also helped us organize the shop.

They painted the inside of the shop and put up shelves. Crawford had nice calligraphy handwriting and he wrote the name of the shop, "The Old Line Shop," on the window boxes. We planted fake boxwood in the window boxes—wired in—with dirt on top. We knew real plants wouldn't grow there. We ran the shop with volunteers for ten years. That shop showed that antique shops were the way to go in town.

Then, the building where we had the Old Line Shop was sold. We asked the new owner if he wanted us to leave—we weren't paying any rent—and he said he did. So, we sold the remaining antiques at auction. Six months after we got rid of everything [Tropical Storm] *Agnes came, and it all would have been destroyed, so we were lucky.*

We formed Historic Ellicott Mills, Inc. and between the profits from the shop and the dues, when we stopped we had about $5,000 in the bank. Jerry Von Mayer in the county planning office helped us a lot—he could see what we saw in Ellicott City. I would be wandering around the halls there a lot when things happened. We had a newsletter called GRIST *and in it we wrote about things nobody talked about, like the slums on Fels Lane with the outhouses.*

[They launched Historic Ellicott Mills, Inc. on February 7, 1962, with the purpose] *to restore and preserve Historic Ellicott Mills through the use of private investment, institutional activities, municipal programs, information and education, community relations, historic area zoning and historic urban renewal.*

When Enalee Bounds and her mother Mrs. Werner came into the shop and introduced themselves and told us that they were leasing the telephone building to use as an antique shop I almost fell off my stool. They were the first real business antique store in town.

Antiques Arrive: Interview with Enalee Bounds

"Growing up in Catonsville and knowing the connection of Catonsville and Ellicott's Mills through the Caton and the Carroll families, I felt right at home when in October of 1962 we opened an antique shop and country store on Main Street," said Enalee Bounds.

Currently the second oldest business on Main Street (after Yates Market), Ellicott's Country Store was emblematic of the sea change that was beginning to occur in the makeup of the town's businesses. Bounds, her mother Mildred Werner and her sister Barbara Baim opened the shop. Bounds continues to run it in the building known as the Walker-Chandler House, built in 1790 and the oldest duplex in Howard County.

Over its long history, the building has been a private home—to Mr. Walker and Mr. Chandler—a boot maker's shop, a funeral home, a tavern, headquarters for the Red Cross and a telephone company office. The ladies who opened Ellicott's Country Store had quite a design challenge to turn the "modern" office décor established by the telephone company back into something more appropriate. Bounds envisioned a shop like the ones she had visited in New England, selling accessories like candles and soap along with the antiques that her mother favored. An old-fashioned display of penny candy completes the mood.

When this shop opened, most of the other businesses in town were utilitarian in nature—grocery stores, barbershops, movie theaters and diners—businesses that would soon find their ways to the newly developing strip shopping malls lining the nearby Baltimore National Pike, Route 40. Only one shop came close to the vision represented by the Country Store, and that was the Old Line Shop, which had opened as a consignment store in 1961.

The Country Store was unique for more than its merchandise—it was also unique in that it was run by women. When they attended their first Business*man*'s Association meeting in town in 1962, they were the only women. Bounds said, "It was predicted that we would only last a couple of months, but all these years later I'm still there. My husband Roland and I purchased the building in 1967 and gradually expanded the business to all four floors."

In 1975, the building next door caught fire and the blaze spread to the shop. A major restoration resulted, uncovering original fireplaces, wood floors and windows. A second fire in 1991 closed the shop for seven months.

Today, nine rooms on four floors offer themes as diverse as the French Country Kitchen and the Nairobi Room.

"What was the town like in 1962?" Bounds recalled.

> *Well, it was a thriving village with grocery stores, a department store, a drugstore, a lumberyard, a hardware store, a furniture store, appliance stores, doctors' and dentists' offices, lunchrooms, a "5 and 10" and many variety stores. It was all very busy with locals, especially on Saturdays when the farmers came to town. There were large beautiful farms and country estates throughout the county.*
>
> *Main Street was a hodgepodge of signs, awnings, parking meters and telephone poles—all the things people thought were necessary to modernize a town. Unless they were stone, most buildings were painted white and turned drab. People seemed to have forgotten the rich history that surrounded the village. The historic buildings were neglected and forlorn. Lots of shops were closed and cried out for loving hands to redo them.*
>
> *There was a small group of people with a vision to bring back the glory and history that seemed to be forgotten. The Howard County Historical Society was founded. Then a group of local history buffs started a paint-up crew and garden club members did their part to try and perk up the rather drab town.*

"In the 1960s, there was no place else to shop in the area, so on Saturdays my father would bring me in to Ellicott City to get my hair cut," said Mike Logan. "I remember being about seven years old and the barber putting the hot shaving foam on the back of my neck for the first time. I remember Cavey's and Votta's."

PRESERVATION SOCIETIES PROLIFERATE: INTERVIEWS WITH CLARE HOEY, JEAN HANNON

In 1957, a group of people interested in organizing a society to investigate and study the history of Howard County and Maryland met in the home of Alda Hopkins Clark. The Howard County Historical Society organized and incorporated as a nonprofit group on December 3. The first officers of the historical society were President Alda Hopkins Clark; Vice-President Louise Kraft Boone; Secretary James F. Cole; and Treasurer Benjamin Mellor Jr.

For two years, the society held meetings in the courthouse and St. John's Episcopal Church. In May 1959, Alda Clark purchased the building that formerly housed the First Presbyterian Church on Court Avenue. Mrs. Clark presented the building to the Howard County Historical Society as a memorial to her late husband, Judge James Clark. The historical society held its first meeting in its new home on September 2, 1959.

Relying solely on membership dues, donations and fundraising projects, the Howard County Historical Society Museum and Library continues to serve those interested in Howard County history. The museum organizes several exhibits and programs a year and is the keeper of an important collection of historical items.

One of the really unusual artifacts on display at the museum is something called a "hairbarium." This consists of locks of hair, often from a child's first

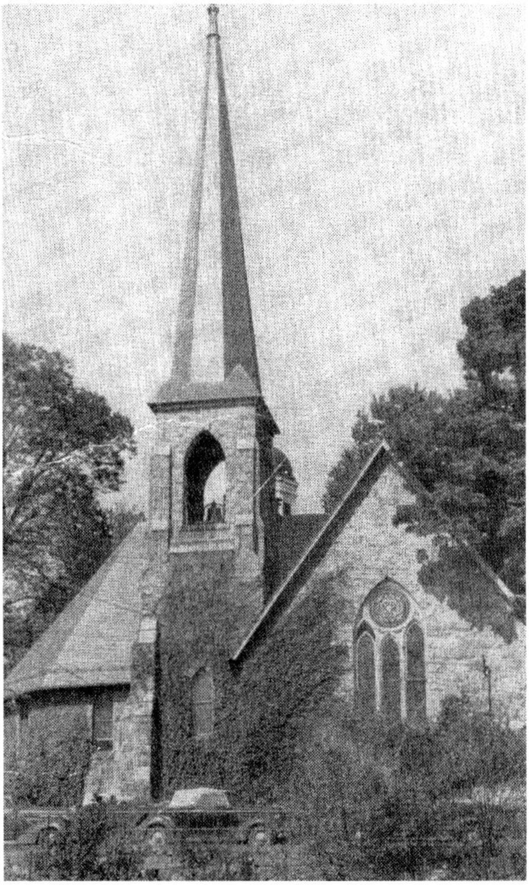

The Howard County Historical Society, housed in a former Presbyterian church. *Courtesy of Victoria Goeller.*

haircut, which are arranged around a picture and labeled with the owner's name. This hairbarium represents members of the Bowie, Gray, Horner, Knight, Knowles, Shepherd, Stinson, Thomas and Warfield families, and the locks date from 1751 to 1867. Martha Ann Knowles made the piece for her niece, Elizabeth Warfield Snowden.

In March 1962, Historic Ellicott Mills began the publication called *GRIST*. Its mission, as stated in the first publication, was:

> *With pending corporate chartering of Historic Ellicott Mills, it was felt that a loud, clear, dependable voice was needed to perpetuate and sustain the interest of everyone who earnestly desires to see this town restored to all the dignity, charm and beauty that had temporarily eluded it. The restoration has begun! Whether you were one of the first to wield a paint brush on that May weekend—made the first cash contribution, may be only slightly interested, or may be shackled by a personal veniality (we'll be patient), we dedicate this sheet to you.*

"Jean Hannon is certainly the godmother to all of the efforts to put the Ellicott City area on the historical map," said Clare Hoey, editor of *GRIST*.

> *In 1960, we all belonged to the Cross Country Garden Club because we weren't old enough or hadn't lived in Howard County long enough to be noticed, that is, by the Howard County Garden Club.*
>
> *The Old Line Shop, the Bell and Quill, all started to make some money to support our cause.* "The Howard County Times" *didn't have much time to get "with us." Along came* "The Central Maryland News," *owned by Irv Cousins, and Editor-cum-laude: Louise (Wese) Hawkins. Now we had a voice and dear old* "GRIST" *was laid to rest. You name it, we, with Jean's prodding, did it. After the big 100 year flood* [Tropical Storm Agnes in 1972] *we petitioned the Baltimore Gas and Electric Company to put the new utility poles underground (no-go: too expensive). We wrote to the Rockefeller brothers who restored Williamsburg to consider helping us. A polite no. Mrs. Werner, Enalee's mother, came along and opened her shop on Main Street and it afforded us more than a modicum of respectability—at last.*

According to *GRIST*, the Bell and Quill opened on March 5, 1962, in the historical society building (which is close to the courthouse), "serving

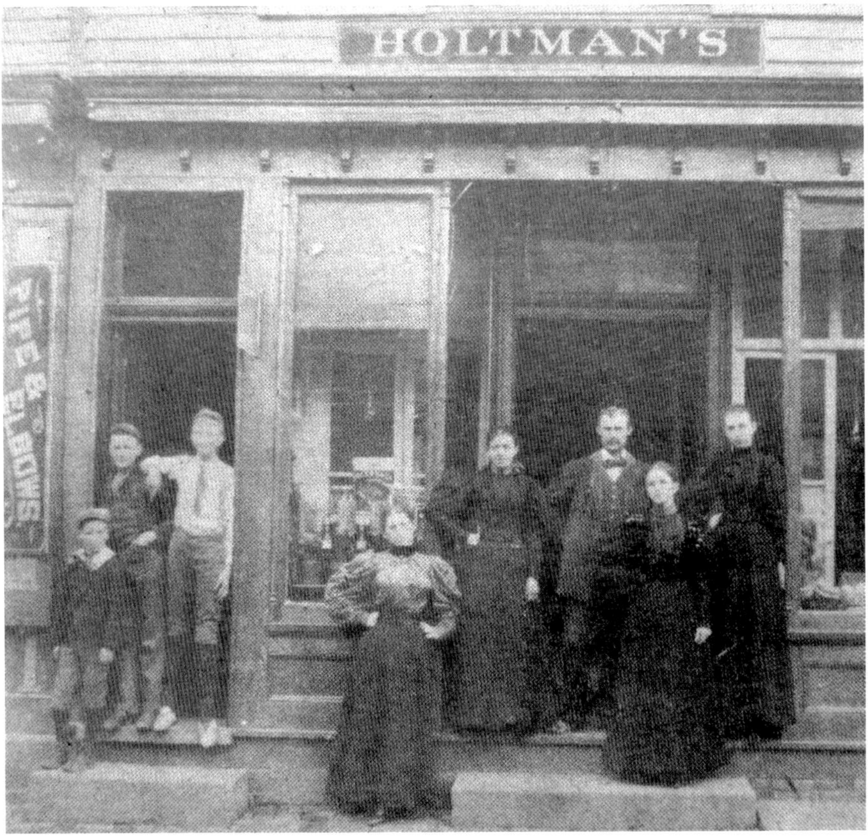

Holtman's store. *Courtesy of Herb Johl.*

luncheon to lawyers, secretaries, clients, politicians, voters and anyone else who happened to be hungry between 11:00 a.m. and 1:00 p.m." Jean Hannon said, "Some friends opened a lunchroom in the historical society, called the 'Bell and Quill.' It opened on the strength of Mrs. McDonald's recipe for Caesar salad. Alda Clark and I were invited for the opening—they served homemade sandwiches and pies. While we were having lunch they started running out of dishes, so Alda and I ended up washing dishes for them."

Meanwhile, at this time, the Old Line Shop was clearing $100 a month, but "more important—has brought a lot of new people into town who are interested in E.C. restoration activities." In April 1962, *GRIST* reported, "Hoopla! The Cupola! The one on the Jail, it's been saved." In April 1963, two years after the paint-the-town event, the paper reported, "Many of the

Main Street merchants have painted their buildings this year and thereby have brightened the area considerably—not to mention our spirits. We hope the merchants will remember that HEM (Historic Ellicott Mills) is still in the color scheme business. PLEASE, no formstone, aluminum awnings, neon signs, or green and brown paint!"

"After the [Old Line] shop closed, Roland Bounds came to see me and asked what and where was Historic Ellicott Mills now," said Hannon.

> *He was getting things going in town, and working to create Historic Ellicott City, Inc. He asked if we could combine Historic Ellicott Mills and Historic Ellicott City, Inc. and we asked our members and that's what we did. I went on to help with the planning of a nicely laid-out historic district and served on the Historic District Commission under both* [County Executives] *Hugh Nichols* [1978–86] *and Liz Bobo* [1986–90]. *The county executive determines a lot about moves in historic preservation.*

At the January 23, 1974 general membership meeting of Historic Ellicott City, Inc., plans for a new publication were unveiled. John Wafer and Rus Wheeler presented their ideas for a monthly newsletter for Historic Ellicott City to be called *Heritage Ellicott City*. Consisting of four pages, the newsletter was to include feature articles, committee reports, general membership meeting minutes and a calendar of events. The cost each month for the publication was $350 for one thousand copies. Revenue from advertising was expected to be $400, providing a profit of $50 each month.

The first edition of *Heritage Ellicott City* arrived in February 1974. The first page featured articles reporting on a survey of the historic district conducted for the Howard County Planning Department and a presentation to be made to the Howard County Zoning Board on February 27, when testimony was to be heard to determine the appropriate boundary for Howard County's *first* historic district.

Inside, a letter from the president, Frederick P. Shultz, congratulated the membership on its approval of the restoration of the B&O Depot. Articles provided information about a membership drive, the "200 Plus 2 Ball" on October 12 at Turf Valley and the successful merger of Historic Ellicott Mills and Historic Ellicott City, Inc. For fifteen years, this free publication provided interesting historical articles, news of restoration and research projects, letters to the editor and updates on the work of Historic Ellicott City, Inc. Enalee Bounds served as editor. It continues to be a valuable resource for information about that time period.

The Welfare Board: Jean Mattern's Memories

In 1961, Jean Mattern went to work at the Welfare Board at the corner of Main Street and Church Road, in the original firehouse. "Mrs. Marshall, as she was always called—(no first names allowed) was the director from 1932 until she retired around 1968," she said.

> *A very bright woman, she grew up in Jessup, went to Randolph-Macon College and graduated at age 18. In many ways she was quite remarkable—had a great relationship with clients, very mindful of their needs—I heard that during the Depression years, she insisted that the staff dress very plainly and she set the example. Even when I was there, she was a little "sticky"—no short skirts—I remember that at that time—there was only one Judge—James McGill—he and Mrs. M. got along famously—Mrs. M never overspent (all very different from today)—as to outside of office time, all of us ate lunch at a combination lunchroom, drug store across the street and Judge McGill ate with us frequently.*
>
> *I found this brief account about the days when the Fire Museum was the Welfare Board—I was a caseworker there in '61–'62, and believe Elizabeth Marshall, the chief, gave this to me when I left:*
>
> *"The Howard County Welfare Board, together with a WPA official moved into the 'old fire house' early in 1935. Formerly they occupied the waiting room of a funeral home and then an apartment over John Votta's shoe repair shop. The fire house had been divided into a waiting room and four offices—partitioned only six feet high so as to get some heat throughout from a kerosene stove in the center. Plumbing pipes ran down the outside wall which meant they were frozen most of the winter. Back steps led from Church Road to Main Street and were used daily by employees 'on the hill' going to and from lunch rooms on lower Main Street. Over the years, the plumbing was improved, central heating was installed and partitions were raised to the ceiling for more privacy in each office—some offices being divided into smaller offices for increased staff which ranged in size from two persons during the World War II years to 10 as increased services were assigned to the department. During the war years a branch of the Howard County public library was set up in the waiting room. In 1962 the Welfare Department vacated the building and moved to larger quarters 'on the hill.'"*

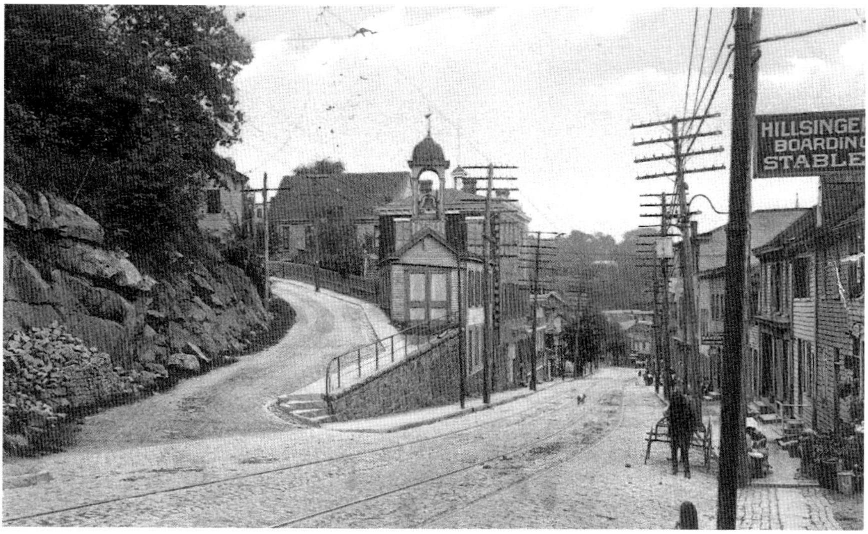

The first firehouse, circa 1909. *Courtesy of Victoria Goeller.*

"This was long before gentrification—Bob's 5 & 10 was great for Christmas stocking stuffers—I don't remember Caplan's but there was a clothing place called Rosenstock's—I used to buy a few items for my children there, but they never thought much about Ellicott City so I put whatever I purchased in a Hutzler's bag [Hutzler's was an upscale Baltimore department store] and they didn't seem to know the difference," said Mattern.

> *Occasionally, the ladies of the church* [now the Historical Society] *served lunch, which was the best ever. There was an M.D., a bank, two drug stores, and an Acme over the bridge—a self-contained community, but many welfare recipients—(will not get into that).*
>
> *I miss E.C. terribly but think I liked the old days the best—Dee's Kitchen, the movie house, etc. No question but that E.C. had a distinct personality—across the street was Eddie's Drug Store and lunch room—frequented by many court employees—also behind the counter Eddie could provide customers with banned books—like Henry Miller's "Tropic of Cancer." He did require that the buyer be of age. Paul's Market was next to the Welfare Board—customers from all over bought their Thanksgiving turkey from Paul. At this point E.C. could provide almost all of your daily needs.*
>
> *I left E.C. to work for the Sisters of Good Shepherd, but still went to E.C. and watched all the changes take place—most positive. One day in*

1971 I noticed a local bookshop on lower Main Street—I stopped in as soon as possible and met George Deeds—a friendly older gentleman who looked as though he had stepped out of a Dickens novel—George was a fascinating person with a very interesting background. I had been collecting books all my life—starting at about age ten when I went to Boston with my mother and we haunted the used bookshops in the Can Hill section of the city. George was determined—although virtually wiped by the [Tropical Storm] *Agnes—he was determined to reopen.*

To summarize—George knew I eventually wanted the shop, and in 1979 George and his wife returned to California and he made good on his promise. Many of the changes that took place in E.C. after I bought the shop have been very well documented. What I felt was truly unique about Deeds were the customers, many of whom became friends. Most were not casual shoppers but people who had a specific interest and their interests were many and varied. The challenge was finding the books for which they were looking. This was not always easy but it gives a real purpose to your life. I tried very hard to keep the shop organized but it was anything but fancy. Nobody seemed to care about that. It was "I want an original Nancy Drew with a perfect dust jacket" or "how come you don't have any more P.Q. Wodehouse." Illustrated children's books were a big item—but they had to have the right illustrations and the right edition—local history, train books. Traveling throughout the country looking for books was my idea of a real vacation.

I do have to admit there was something about the old Ellicott City I loved—Dee's Kitchen, Paul's Market, the Commercial and Farmers Bank, Alda's Fabric Shop, and the cozy library where the Welfare Board used to be. Fortunately the Country Store is still with us. There is currently a very fine book store in E.C.—Gramp's Attic—at the top of the hill across from the copy shop. Walter Jackson, the owner, has some wonderful books, and has a fascinating shop.

Janet Kusterer shopped at Deeds when Mattern owned it. "I went in there looking for a copy of Celia Holland's book *Ellicott City, Maryland—Mill Town USA*," said Kusterer. "The only copy Jean had was battered and missing pages. She sold it to me at a discount, and Xeroxed the missing pages for me from her own copy. She never forgot—a few years later she came across an intact copy, called me and we traded. I had to pay a little more for the good copy, but it was worth it."

WRITING ABOUT THE TOWN: INTERVIEW WITH CHARLOTTE HOLLAND

Charlotte Holland's mother, Celia Holland, wrote extensively about Ellicott City in the 1960s and 1970s. In the 1960s, Charlotte accompanied her to many of the places she ended up writing about. "It was a great deal of fun," said Charlotte.

> *My mother once heard a friend say that "oh, they just oughta burn that place down." Well, he got a lecture from my mother about the historic value of Ellicott City. She thought the architecture was so unique. She started writing articles—reviewing and photographing some of the old buildings—for the* Central Maryland News, *where Louise Hawkins was editor. She later did the same thing for the* Howard County Times *under Doris Thompson.*

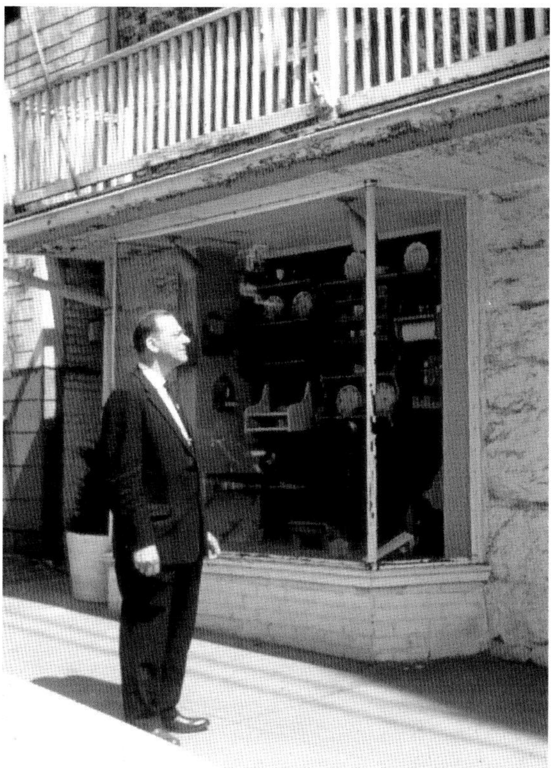

Sam Caplan. *Courtesy of Herb Johl.*

> *Occasionally, I would come up with her on the weekend and we'd review the building that she was currently interested in, and it always involved talking with some of the old-timers—Mildred Werner, and of course Enalee* [Bounds—Mildred's daughter]. *Sam Caplan—I remember him very well. He was a big help to my mom and he loved to tell stories about Ellicott City. And I mean mom would just bubble—a big grin on her face, writing everything down—very, very excited about the old town. Fortunately her articles were well received, and about the same time the preservationists here in Ellicott City were beginning to get together and organize and mom became one of them. Her interest eventually led to her book* Ellicott City, Maryland—Mill Town USA *in 1970.*

All was not rosy in Ellicott City at this time. There was a problem in town much more serious than the perennial lack of adequate parking. In 1963, parts of the town were declared a slum, lacking proper sewerage—raw sewage was simply dumped into the river—and featuring poor wiring, leaky roofs and crumbling plaster. Although the entire Main Street area from the Patapsco River to Fels Lane was included, much of the substandard housing was found on Fels Lane and was subsequently torn down to make way for a parking lot.

Transitions: Memories of Lisa Peklo and Ned Rogers

"It was 1973 when my 16-year-old sister Anne Tumulty visited our young married's apartment on West Springs Drive in Ellicott City," said Lisa Peklo. "We decided to hike down into the historic district to soak up the Main Street atmosphere. Somewhere along Rogers Avenue, a hot rod, filled with rowdies who spoke with a twang from beyond, pulled up alongside us and asked, 'Do you girlies know the way to Elegant City?' Since that day we never refer to this beloved town as anything but Elegant City."

The '70s were a time of real transition for Ellicott City. People who lived in town in their young adulthood then are now referred to as baby boomers, and they vividly remember their experiences.

"Although my father's family goes way back in Ellicott City, I was never more than a visitor until the early '70s," said Dr. Edward "Ned" Rogers, a psychologist who practiced in the historic district for many years.

The town was a little different in character and characters back then, a good deal closer to a time when you might not bring up the fact that you lived there, rather than stretch a point and claim that you did.

Among the denizens of Main Street at that time was Henry Butler. A modestly but always nattily turned out older black man, he would sidle up to just about anyone standing still and begin by crooning "Moohnah Lisa, Mona Lisa men have named you…" which I didn't realize until years later was an homage to Nat King Cole. The conversation usually didn't go much past that, but there was plenty of it. He could go into great detail about nothing in particular, and if you had nothing to do (or say) it was quite congenial. People like Henry made us feel pretty grownup, partly because we had jobs sometimes and he didn't, but also because we were in a real community. A real poor, dysfunctional community in many ways, but still a real live place.

The Trolley Stop was of course known as "The Bloody Bucket," and long-hairs such as my confreres and I were then would be unwise to wander over there alone. At that time, and even 10 years later, everything that you needed was within walking distance on Main Street. There was a fair share of merchants survived from when Ellicott City was important as the County seat, and served as the place where a farmer would need to go at the end of the week to buy things city people take for granted. Or get liquored up, as the case might be. Caplan's of course served as the department store, appliances, clothing, though most of it out of date by our time, paint, etc.

Still, the town was an agreeable locale for us, since then as now denizens tended to be independent and generous with their opinions. For instance, Valmas was a small store at the location of the present Phoenix. On the door of the store was a prominent hand-lettered sign that said, "No we DO NOT HAVE any FILM." Then there was Votta's shoe repair (which had once been the headquarters for the infamous Sheriff Wosch), cleaners, Rock Hill Liquors (who would cash my paycheck when the bank wouldn't), Yates Hardware and Yates Grocery (SJ Yates and Son, and the grandson Bladen was on his way to eighty). But my favorite was Paul's grocery. The store had a big awning out front that covered wooden bins that were filled with shaved ice and whole fish, etc. A big red and white rusted Sealtest sign was overtop and the wooden floors inside showed the wear of many thousands of shuffling in and out by those who had gone before. Super Fresh it was not. Super real it was.

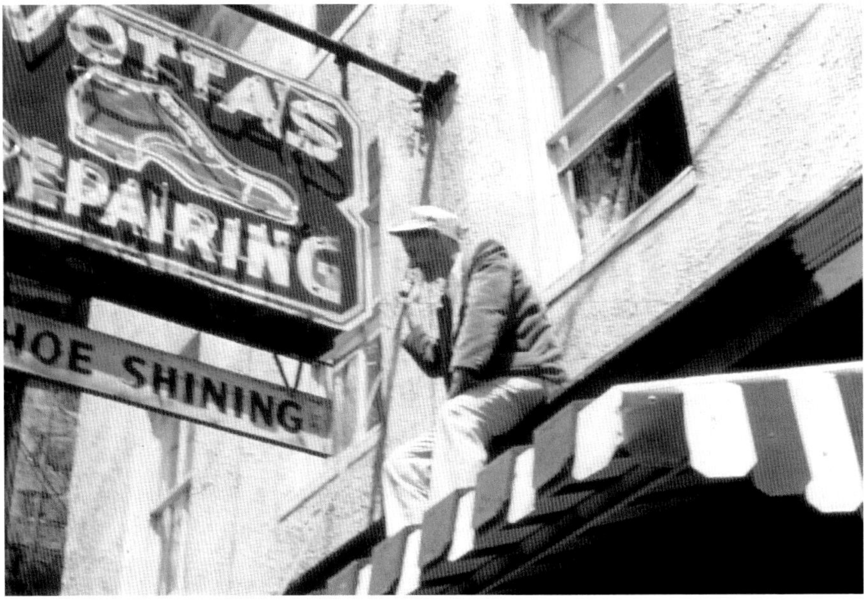

Votta's Shoe Repair. *Courtesy of Herb Johl.*

We made almost enough money to break even. Fortunately we had Sam Caplan as a landlord, and he understood sometimes the first of the month arrives a little before payday. Sam Caplan was a kind man, and a benevolently neglectful landlord (later called a one man social welfare agency by Don Reuwer when he "remodeled" Main Street). Between him and relative by marriage Isaac Taylor (who owned a large furniture store just up the corner—and a mental hospital) they quietly controlled most of Ellicott City real estate.

Interview with Jared Spahn

"I was the eighth baby born at Howard County General Hospital," said Jared Spahn.

My father worked as a lawyer on Park Avenue in Ellicott City with Charles Wehland. The Caplans and the Taylors came to them to help set up their business merger as Historic Ellicott Properties. Charles became the lawyer for the Caplans and my father became the lawyer for the Taylors. My parents each lost their father at a young age, my father lost his mother when I was seven and my mom's mother lived out of town. Sam and Gertrude Caplan didn't have any grandchildren and enjoyed being around children, so my sister and I spent a lot of time with them and they were our surrogate grandparents. We are Jewish and they were, too, so they would tell us about the ten Jewish families who owned shops on Main Street at the turn of the twentieth century. Once in Sunday school, we had to write about a famous Jewish person. Most kids picked Golda Meir or Elie Wiesel. I wrote about Sam Caplan.

When they would come to our house to dinner, Sam would often bring me a roll of coins to help with my coin collection. He had a variety of safes in his basement and could never remember the combinations, so would have to call in someone to open them for him, and he would get the coins out for me. About one night a month, when my parents wanted to go out, my sister and I would spend the night at the Caplans' home, which was over their store. They had a chairlift to the second floor, which we loved to ride. Their apartment included a small foyer, a dining room, kitchen and living room with a small television with rabbit ears. Family photos were everywhere. It's amazing to me that I now own that building.

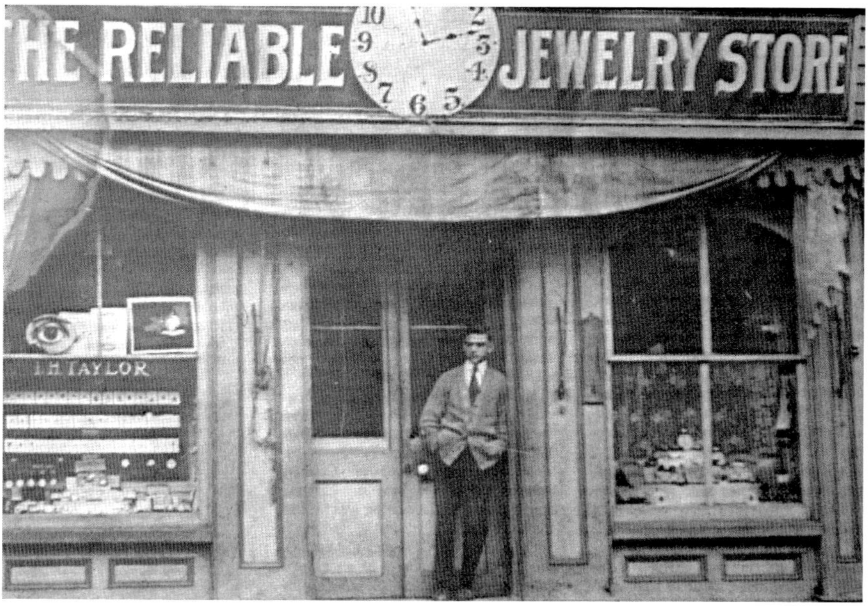

Isaac Taylor. *Courtesy of Herb Johl.*

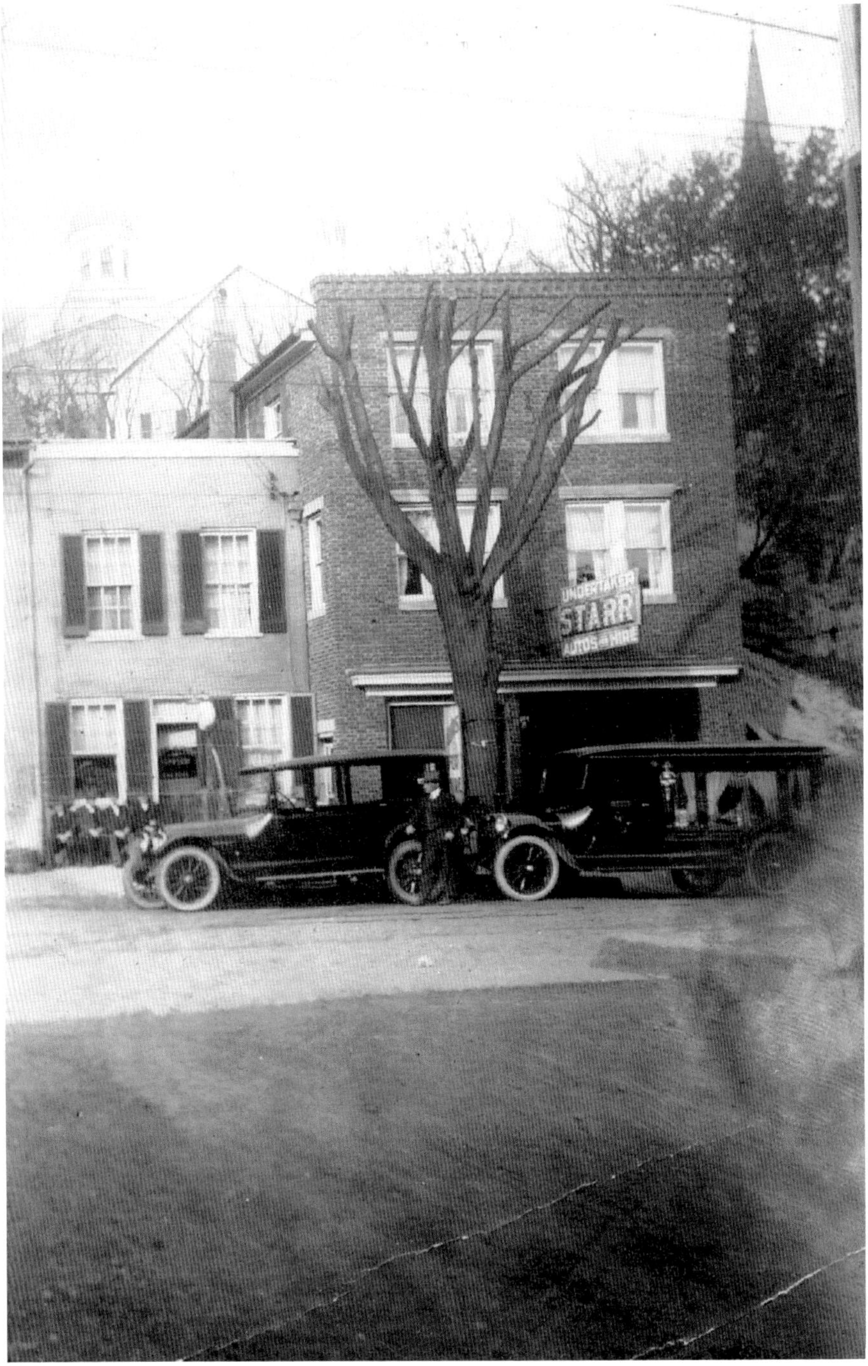

Starr Funeral Home. *Courtesy of Herb Johl.*

The Rosenstock Building that my company rebuilt after the fire of 1999 was my fourth restoration or construction project on Main Street. The third was the conversion of the Commercial and Farmers Bank into space for Creative Access. The second was the building behind La Palapa Restaurant on the parking lot behind the post office, and the first was when I was five years old. My father, Ronald Spahn, worked with Charles Wehland and Don Reuwer and often brought me along to help out. They were restoring the building that had housed the Starr Funeral Home. They bought it, planned to fix it up and then lease it. This was twenty-nine years ago. Don was thirty, my father was forty and Charles was fifty. This was typical of Ellicott City history—fathers teaching the business to their sons. My job then was to run to Yates Market or Dee's Kitchen for sandwiches, or to Talbott's Lumber for a board or some nails. I can't walk by the Brewing Company (where Talbott's was) without thinking of stopping in for some nails. My nickname was Bo, and when I went in and asked for a piece of wood, they'd say, "Bo, just go on back in the yard and find what you need." Today's commercial buildings are often a mix of retail, office space and residential. Ellicott City has been like that since 1772. I think we're coming to an end of that phase of Ellicott City history. That initial concept has ended—we're less self-contained now.

After Talbott's Lumber closed, the Ellicott Mills Brewing Company opened in 1997 as a restaurant and microbrewery and was recognized by the Historic District Commission for the quality of its renovation. The building, constructed in 1905, is the only hand-carved granite edifice in the historic district. The copper kettles used in the brewing process are from the Czech Republic and can brew 620 gallons of beer at a time. The brewery creates a German-style lager in a process that goes from the kettles to fermenting tanks to lager "tuns" for a second fermentation. The entire process takes about a month. In contrast, ales can be prepared in as little as a week. The building is a fine example of historic preservation in the district.

A New Shop and a Late-night Club: Interviews with John Beck and James Robey

John Beck first moved to the historic district in March 1972, when he lived and worked in a building on Tongue Row, Old Columbia Pike. Tongue Row,

row houses built in the nineteenth century, has such a period feel that in 2000 the Learning Channel used it as a backdrop when filming *Les Miserables* for its *Great Books* television series.

"Ellicott City was a very viable small town in 1972, when I first arrived," said Beck.

> *It was a living, working town with facilities and services and day-to-day necessities. There were three grocery stores—Yates, Paul's and the Villa; there was a hardware store, a shoemaker, movie theater (which closed after the flood—Agnes—even though the building wasn't damaged), two banks, two drugstores, two department stores—Taylor's and Caplan's—and the bakery. At the department stores, they would keep your tab and you would pay what you could in cash and they would give you a receipt.*
>
> *There were many families residing in town—people who worked at the mill—and lots of kids around. It was an intact, contained place. In 1972, I opened a "head" shop called the Front Room. The Tongue Row building where I lived and had my shop was a small stone structure—the shop was on the middle level, with a kitchen at the lowest level and two bedrooms and bath on the top floor. My rent was about $175 per month. Shops on Tongue Row at the time featured antiques, imported products and vintage clothes. I closed the shop after less than two years because I wasn't making very much money—and I was ready for a change.*
>
> *Later on in the '70s, I worked in the box office of Super Star, a disco located at the corner of Main Street and Columbia Pike. It was an after-hours club, complete with membership cards, sited there to attract people on their way home from clubs in Baltimore and Washington, D.C. The building next door housed a sandwich shop with a few tables so people could get something to eat, but there was no on-site alcohol. On Friday and Saturday nights, it was always mobbed, and people could dance until four in the morning. There was a Plexiglas dance floor with lights underneath that moved to the music, and a large movie screen that displayed light shows as well. It was great.*

James Robey was a rookie police officer at the time. "I joined the police department in June of 1966," he said.

> *The police station was located on Fels Lane behind the fire department. Technology was not a big part of being a police officer then. We had a radio in the car, but if we left the car we didn't have anything. I walked*

foot patrol on Main Street. One time, around three or four in the morning, I was walking and heard a tremendous crash that really scared me. It turned out to be a big raccoon.

Ellicott City was not so upscale and affluent then. There were disorderly people around. For a while there was "Club Super Star" where the old movie used to be. After midnight, the crowd would leave the club and some would hang around outside. One time I had to subdue a patron. I was working alone and trying to put handcuffs on him, and I suddenly felt a cold rush of air and heard a lady say, "That officer's pants ripped." All I could think of is my mother's admonition to always wear clean underwear.

Chapter 6

FOUNDATIONS FOR THE FUTURE

INTERVIEW WITH THE TERSIGUEL FAMILY

Fernand Tersiguel, his wife Odette and son Michel have been part of the fabric of Main Street for most of the past four decades. First with Chez Fernand, which opened in 1975, and later with Tersiguel's French Country Restaurant, they have been a part of the town movement away from its utilitarian phase to its current status as a shopping, dining and entertainment destination point.

"The first time I came to Main Street in Ellicott City was during the Bicentennial of the town in 1972, when I cooked crepes on the sidewalk in front of the Tiber River Inn," said Fernand Tersiguel.

> *At that time there were only two restaurants in town—the Inn and Dee's Kitchen, so they didn't mind that I was there too. I was there from Papillion restaurant (a French restaurant that was just outside the historic district, now torn down to make way for housing), and I already knew a lot of people in Ellicott City from working at Papillion.*
>
> *We weren't sure that Ellicott City would be a good fit for a restaurant for us, but the Tiber River Inn came up for sale and we were able to buy it, and it became Chez Fernand. We opened on July 14, 1975—Bastille Day—and were open seven days a week. We had six employees at the time so we had to do most everything ourselves. Our dishwasher was a very nice seventy-year-old lady. The first day we finished work at 4:00 a.m. and I was back at 7:00 a.m. the same day. In the first six months, I*

> *only took one half-day off, and Odette and I went to dinner at Cacao Lane Restaurant. Cate Olsen was president of the Business Association for a long time around then, and she started the festivals we used to have in town. Also, in 1977 and '78 we held waiters' races on Main Street, with the street closed to traffic.*

"We created everything inside the restaurant," said Odette Tersiguel.

> *There were linoleum floors, and the most expensive thing in the restaurant was a pewter rooster. One day someone stole it. We couldn't believe it. In the beginning, I remember cooking onion soup at 3:00 a.m. I did most of the cooking, and Fernand did the meat preparation, cleaned the salad greens and made all the dressings and sauces. The menu featured veal forestiere, poulet champagne, fillet of sole, crepes and onion soup. We bought our fish from Paul's Market on Main Street. The chicken dish cost $4.25 and the veal was $6.25. It was a different town then. We knew everyone and everyone was very friendly. Of course they are still friendly today; it's just different.*

"I started working at the restaurant when I was eleven years old," said Michel Tersiguel.

> *I remember that the table bases were old sewing machines. People would rock their feet back and forth on the treadles. The chairs were antiques and every one was different. I washed dishes twelve hours a day, and when I got tired I slept on the bags of dirty linen. I was also the doorman and bouncer for the restaurant. I wore a bow tie and stood at the front door, and I was the first alarm if bums were trying to get in. I also remember the basement—there was a small hole where you could see out to the river* [a feature common to buildings on the south side of the street].

One of the worst fires in Ellicott City history occurred on November 14, 1984. It began in the rear of Leidig's Bakery and quickly spread to the adjacent Chez Fernand Restaurant and then to Ye Olde Towne Clock and Watch Shoppe, Marino's Art Galleries, Chateau Wine Supply and the Iron Rail. Fighting what became a six-alarm blaze was difficult due to the presence of the Tiber-Hudson Branch of the river immediately behind the buildings. After the fire, all the buildings were declared unsafe and were razed.

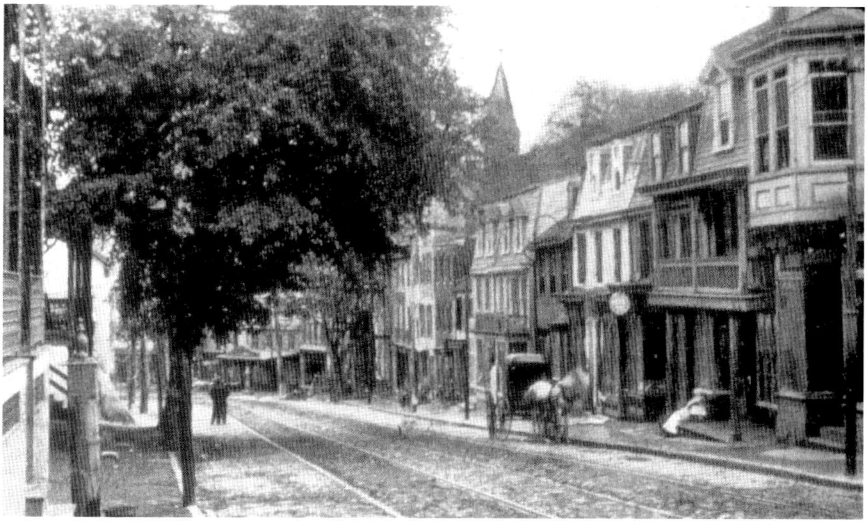

Early view of the site of the 1984 fire. *Courtesy of Herb Johl.*

Damages were estimated to be $1.3 million. Nine apartment occupants were displaced but no one was seriously injured.

"The fire of November 14, 1984, destroyed our restaurant, Chez Fernand," said Fernand.

> *It was the day before we were to celebrate the arrival of the Nouveau Beaujolais wine. At around 10:00 p.m., we started to smell smoke and walked all around the building trying to find the source. The fire had started next door, at Leidig's Bakery, and when we realized it we had about five minutes to get out. We were worried about the person who lived in the apartment above Leidig's but everyone got out safely. I didn't sleep for three days—Ellicott City was never as busy as during that cleanup—everyone came to town to watch.*

"We worked so hard and then we lost everything," said Odette.

Michel was attending the Culinary Institute of America in Hyde Park, New York, when the fire happened. He said, "My father called me the next morning and said, 'Something terrible has happened.' He sounded so sad that I immediately thought my mother had died. That put the news of the fire in perspective for me—it was bad but wasn't the worst that could happen."

"We wanted to reopen but couldn't find a place in Ellicott City—they wanted $3 million for Papillion and we couldn't afford that—so in 1985 we moved to Baltimore, near the Shot Tower, where we stayed for five years," remembered Fernand.

> *When we were ready to come back to Ellicott City, I thought I wanted to rent space rather than buy, but in partnership with Don Reuwer I was able to buy our current building, and within a year I owned it. Our current building was first the home of Dr. Sykes and his family, built in 1895. In the 1930s, it was divided into three apartments, and around 1947 it became the office of the Health Department. In the 1980s, it became business offices.*

Born in Ellicott's Mills on January 13, 1860, Mordecai Sykes followed his father, Sylvanus, into the dental profession. Sylvanus continued to practice dentistry until his death in 1872. An ad for Dr. Sylvanus Sykes in the *Howard County Gazette* in 1849 reads:

> *S. Sykes*
> *Surgeon Dentist, Ellicotts' Mills*
> *Continues to attend to the various diseases of the Teeth and Gums, and restore them to their natural beauty and soundness. Teeth extracted with the most approved instruments, and the least possible pain.*
> *Teeth plugged with Gold & Silver Foil. Also artificial Teeth inserted on pivot, Gold and Silver plate, with neatness and comfort to the wearer, on the most reasonable terms.*
> *Residence 2d door from Mr. J. Forrest's Store.*
> *April 21st.*

Committed to public service, Dr. Mordecai Sykes, a Democrat, was first elected mayor of Ellicott City in April 1889. He declined the nomination in 1891, and was again elected mayor in 1893. Dr. Sykes is reported to have traveled to his office at Springfield State Hospital in Sykesville twice a month on a bicycle, a distance of over sixteen miles each way.

Dr. Sykes remained absorbed in matters having to do with Main Street. In 1922, it was rumored that shade trees on the western end of Main Street were to be removed during the construction of a new state road through Ellicott City. Rallying to save the trees, Dr. Sykes proclaimed, "It would be a disgrace and detriment to the town to have these trees removed. I cannot see where the road would be benefited by the removal of my tree, and it shall not be removed without a kick on my part." Much to the relief of Dr. Sykes and others in Ellicott City, the state roads committee announced that removal of the trees was not necessary.

INTERVIEW WITH GEORGE GOELLER

"In 1978, I owned a bar in Fells Point [in Baltimore], the Horse You Came In On, with a partner," said George Goeller.

> *I sold my half of the business to my partner and began looking for a new location. An accountant friend of mine wanted me to invest in a skateboard park in the Woodlawn, Social Security, area. He conducted a demographic study and discovered there was a high population in the area. I had looked at a couple properties in Baltimore, but with the new information I widened my search.*
>
> *I had been through Ellicott City and had an interest in antiques and old buildings. In Fells Point, I served on the board of directors of the Preservation Society of Federal Hill and Fells Point. I'd been out of the Horse for a couple of months and needed to do something. The auction of the Maryland Inn came up. No one had a saloon/restaurant in Ellicott City, and I wanted to sell light fare.*
>
> *I believe the auction was held on November 21, 1978. I knew the auctioneer, Alex Cooper, from buying antiques. There were three groups of serious buyers. Dr. Irvin Taylor, accompanied by Sam Caplan, was one of the bidders. Dr. Taylor and I were bidding against each other. As the bidding continued, Sam Caplan kept telling Dr. Taylor to go ahead and bid one more time, hoping I was out of money. Sam was right—I was at the end. If Dr. Taylor had bid once more, I would have had to drop out of the bidding. I outlasted Dr. Taylor and won the auction. A $10,000 deposit was required in cash or cashiers check. I had $9,999 in cash and had to borrow a dollar from Bruce, the auctioneer.*
>
> *The Maryland Inn was located at the corner of Maryland Avenue and Main Street. A husband, wife and their son-in-law purchased it from the Valmas family after Tropical Storm Eloise in 1975. They renovated the interior, which was damaged during Eloise. The husband had been the driving force of the project, but after his death the business never opened and the liquor license expired.*

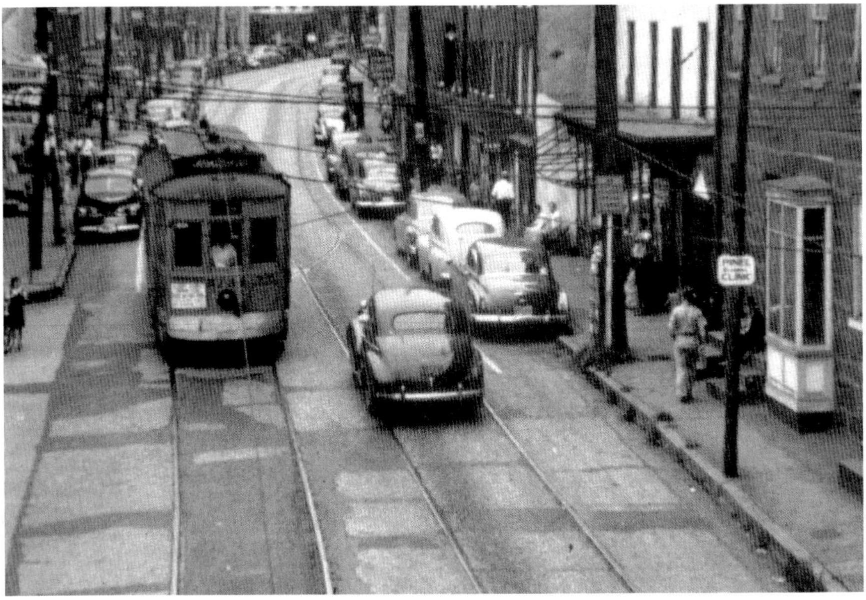

Main Street and Maryland Avenue. *Courtesy of Herb Johl.*

Some of the merchants and residents had serious reservations about me, the longhaired guy from Fells Point. They were concerned about what kind of business I would run and contested my liquor license. I shaved, got a haircut and got the liquor license.

I went to settlement in January 1979 and began renovations. I used the same group of guys who worked at the Horse. The floor was rotten and the air conditioning that was supposed to work didn't. We built a trapdoor in the floor behind the bar and lowered beer in a milk crate into the river so we didn't have to turn on the beer coolers. We used Talbott's Lumber Company for everything. During that time, I met Al Parsons who owned Cacao Lane, Steve Hargest who worked for Al and later owned Side Streets, John Beck, the bartender at Cacao Lane and attorney Pres Pairo.

Some of the businesses that were operating on Main Street were my neighbor—Ray's Villa Market, Paul's Market, Chez Fernand, the Kitchen Basket, Dee's Kitchen, the Owl and the Pussycat, Baxter's, Taylor's and Ellicott's Country Store.

I had two ideas for names, Buffalo Chips or the Phoenix Emporium. I chose the Phoenix Emporium because the phoenix represented rebirth and an emporium was a store that sold a multitude of things, and I wanted to buy and sell antiques. I thought an artist could make a nice logo out of the phoenix. If I had known the business had been called O'Brien's, I would have called it O'Brien's Saloon. That name would have guaranteed a great St. Patrick's Day party every year. I hoped the business would be known as the Emporium but everyone called it the Phoenix.

I opened on July 19, 1979. The general manager was John Read, who now owns the Old Mill Bakery Café. My first chef had just returned from San Diego and the menu, which was written on a chalkboard, included crepes, burgers, onion soup, chili, sandwiches, shrimp salad, brie and quiche. I used my mother's recipe and served Mrs. G's crab cakes. We served fifty imported beers. The Phoenix was a success from the start. The majority of our customers were restaurant workers who stopped in after work. We had some great events: toga and pajama parties, Halloween costume parties, anniversary and Christmas parties. I had a friend, Michael Englestad, who was a professional photographer. He would photograph all the parties and give me the slides. I installed a screen at the end of the bar and would show the slides at events every year. In the beginning, John Read and I lived upstairs. After a couple of years, I purchased a house on Court Avenue.

Parking was always a problem in Ellicott City. One year the county announced they were going to paint spaces on Main Street. The spaces were going to be big, twenty-three foot or something. I was the vice-president of the Business Association. We tried to convince the county the spaces were too big, we'd lose spaces. But the county went ahead and painted the lines anyway—they were huge, way too big. I got a can of black spray paint and with Cate Olsen as the lookout we went out at four-thirty in the morning and I painted over the lines from the Forget-Me-Not Factory east to the bridge. There was room for a lot more cars and the county never came back to repaint the lines.

I remember a flood in the fall of 1979 or '80. The Howard County Police told me I had to close. I told them I didn't think they had the authority to do that. I told them to get the liquor inspector to tell me to close. There was water in the street and when it crested the curb we began to move furniture, liquor, beer and the register upstairs. We watched the storm from the porch. During the fire of 1984, we helped the owners of Act I and II move their inventory of women's clothing and stored it on the second floor of the Phoenix.

Customers used to leave all kinds of belongings at the Phoenix; we must have had about one hundred umbrellas. Every year the B&O Museum had a haunted house tour at Halloween time. One year there were about fifty people standing in line outside when there was a surprise downpour. I remembered all the umbrellas. My wife, Vickie, and I took them over to the people standing in line. They thought there was a catch, that we were selling umbrellas. After convincing them there was no catch we handed out forty-seven umbrellas. The next morning, lined up in a row on the second-floor balcony were the forty-seven umbrellas. Every umbrella was returned!

Over the years the Phoenix became a meeting place for people. We never closed. We were open on Christmas Eve, and every year friends home from college or who had moved away would meet there. You could stop by the Phoenix on Thanksgiving or Christmas night and find friends. If you were snowed in on Main Street you could walk to the Phoenix for a beer or a burger. Although I sold the business to Mark Hemmis in 2001, I still own the building and I'm thankful I won the bidding that day in November 1978.

Interview with Barry Gibson

The Opera House is the tallest building on Main Street and in its two centuries of existence has served as a place of entertainment, the town hall, a grocery store and a furniture store. For the past three decades, it has been home to the Forget-Me-Not Factory. Its owners, Barry and Nancy Gibson, have worked on Main Street since the early 1980s and lived there since 1990.

"My wife Nancy and I came to Ellicott City in 1983," said Gibson.

Nancy was working trade shows in her business and wanted to expand by opening a shop, the Forget-Me-Not Factory. She first opened on Main Street where Carpe Vinum is now. In 1985, the owner of the Opera House nearby, Andy Bibo, offered to sell it to us and we decided to buy it. At first we used only the first floor as everything needed to be restored. Over time we put in new utilities, floors and plumbing. During our restoration work we've uncovered a variety of artifacts including bottles, Victorian shoes, plates and coins. I found a 1789 Continental gold coin in one of the fireplaces. One time I poked a hole in the ceiling and a bunch of Bennington marbles fell out. I suspect that a child had put them into the heat register in the floor above.

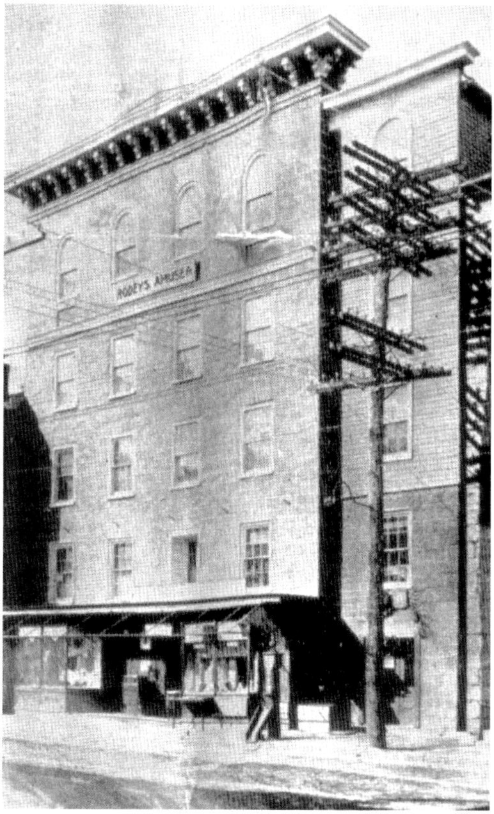

Rodey's Amusea, now the Forget-Me-Not Factory. *Courtesy of Herb Johl.*

For a while we rented space on the second floor to individual businesses, but in 1989 we decided to expand our own business to the second floor. In 1993, we added the space on the third floor, and use the fourth floor, which is where the performances were held, for storage. My wife and her mother, Janet Vanderlipp, run the business. I'm involved in marketing and promotion.

Jonathan Ellicott once lived in the building, until he moved across the river to a house next door to his brother George, next to their mill. The Opera House has triangular hewn stone inserts above the windows which are similar to those on the George Ellicott House. It wasn't until the 1850s that the fourth-floor theatre was added on to our building. During the Civil War, the provost marshal's office was located in the building, and it also housed prisoners. There is a popular myth that John Wilkes Booth performed there, but that isn't true. He went to school at St. Timothy's in nearby Catonsville and probably hung out in Ellicott City occasionally, but he would have been about fourteen at the time.

> *Vaudeville shows and opera were performed there. One time while I was blowing bubbles on the street, I met a woman who had played the piano in the theatre when they showed silent movies. The piano is still there, and dates from before the 1880s. The man who ran the silent movies lived in the adjacent dressing room, which still has coat hooks on the walls. In the early 1900s, Ed Rodey owned the building, called then an Amusea, which he outfitted with a variety of entertainment, including a bowling alley.*

An 1898 advertisement from Gibson's collection promoted a "Grand Carnival of Novelties" to be held on Tuesday, May 3, at the "Assembly Room, Ellicott City," which was on the fourth floor of the building. The event was a fundraiser for the Lutheran Church and featured acts included a zither solo, a statuary grouping and something called "a pathetic tableau—the little outcasts." Tickets were twenty-five cents for general admission, thirty-five cents for reserved seats. The ad promised "all features blended with calcium light effects."

"In 1990, we bought and moved into the town house next door, which dates from the early nineteenth century," said Gibson.

> *The house also had to be totally restored. We took out all the old lumber, redid and replaced the brick work and replaced two brick fireplaces with brick from the Phoenix Emporium across the street.*
>
> *I always enjoyed being the store greeter and always did costumed characters. In 1987, Nancy went to a trade show in California and came back with bubble products, which she asked me to demonstrate. I've blown bubbles in front of the store ever since. I once was on CNN as a "Crime Stopper Bunny." Two people came into the store and they were obnoxious and loud. I happened to be wearing a bunny costume at the time. I thought they were shoplifting but wasn't sure, so I decided to follow them up the street. I watched them in the shop next door, the Crystal Underground, and determined that they were indeed shoplifting. When they left that shop, I went in and told the owner to call the police and tell them to look for a bunny standing outside a shop on Main Street. I ended up following them up the street about a block and couldn't believe they didn't notice a man in a bunny costume outside every store they went in.*
>
> *There have been many nice events in town over the years I have been here. In 1990, we celebrated the Beaujolais Nouveau arrival in style—the wine*

> *was dropped into a parking lot from a helicopter, and then delivered around town by horse and carriage.* [The Beaujolais Nouveau tradition began in Paris in the 1950s. The wine is never released to the public until the third Thursday of November every year, and it indicates what the year's vintage will be like.]
>
> *The Ellicott City Business Association partnered with Howard County Recreation and Parks for another popular event, the May Arts Fest, which started in 1983 and lasted in town for ten years, eventually becoming "Wine in the Woods"—a popular event held yearly in Symphony Woods in Columbia. We simply ran out of room in town. Caryl Maxwell, who had a ballet studio on Main Street, organized a Maypole dance.*

"We also did a 'Millfest' in the summer in the late 1980s into the '90s," said Gibson. This event included artists and artisans, horse-drawn carriage rides, historic interpreters, pony rides, tours and special exhibits. One really popular event was the waiters' race, a true test of endurance and balance. Waiters from local restaurants would race while carrying trays that they would have to add items to as they moved down the street from the Log Cabin to the Railroad Station Plaza.

For over thirty years, the Christmas season has hit high gear in the historic district on the first Friday in December, an event affectionately called "Midnight Madness." Back when it started, in the 1970s, it was Tim Moran's idea to have a special night when the shops would stay open late to accommodate holiday shoppers. His wife Loretta had a shop on Main Street called the Dandyline, and she presented the idea to the Ellicott City Business Association. Many of the shop owners were members, and so many participated in the event, sending out direct mailings to their customers and assisting with advertising. The fun includes Santa's arrival by fire truck, carolers and music.

"It took a while for Midnight Madness to get off the ground," said Gibson.

> *We built on it in the 1980s. We got a lot of attention from television, radio and the newspapers. I dressed up like Father Christmas and went on television to promote it. A few years ago we had a problem with teenage kids hanging around in Tiber Alley, while we wanted a family event. So, we thought about what kids don't like and decided to broadcast classical music. We had a DJ at the Railroad Station Plaza*

and he knew exactly what we were doing—and it worked, the kids left and families returned. These days we have expanded the event to be a hospitality weekend to kick off the holiday season in the historic district.

Routine Maintenance

Old towns, like all old things, need constant maintenance. In 1992, the county created a "pocket park" where the old Earle Theatre used to be, on the south side of lower Main Street. For many years, the spot featured a cinderblock wall that hid a garbage-strewn empty lot. During the construction work, crews unearthed a variety of things, including liquor bottles with corks still in them (the site once housed a saloon) and coins. Tiber Park has a brick-lined footbridge over the Tiber Branch of the river, picnic tables and a small garden. It is the smallest park in the Howard County park system.

In 1997, Columbia Pike was closed for five months so that the river channel running under the road could be repaired. A portion of the road is actually a bridge over the Tiber-Hudson Branch of the Patapsco, visible in the former post office parking lot but underground elsewhere. The running water exerts pressure on the retaining concrete walls, and if they aren't properly maintained the street could collapse. At the same time, the county constructed the steep ramp that leads from the former post office parking lot to Columbia Pike.

Directly behind the Thomas Isaac Log Cabin, at the corner of Main Street and Ellicott Mills Drive, is a small stone building that once served as Ellicott City's first courthouse, from 1840 to 1843, while the large courthouse up the hill was being built. On August 21, 1998, Historic Ellicott City, Inc. celebrated the grand opening of a special exhibit created in the building, which was called the Heritage Orientation Center. This small building holds a wealth of information about the fires, floods and Ellicott family that all shaped the town we know today. Displays include photographs and a timeline.

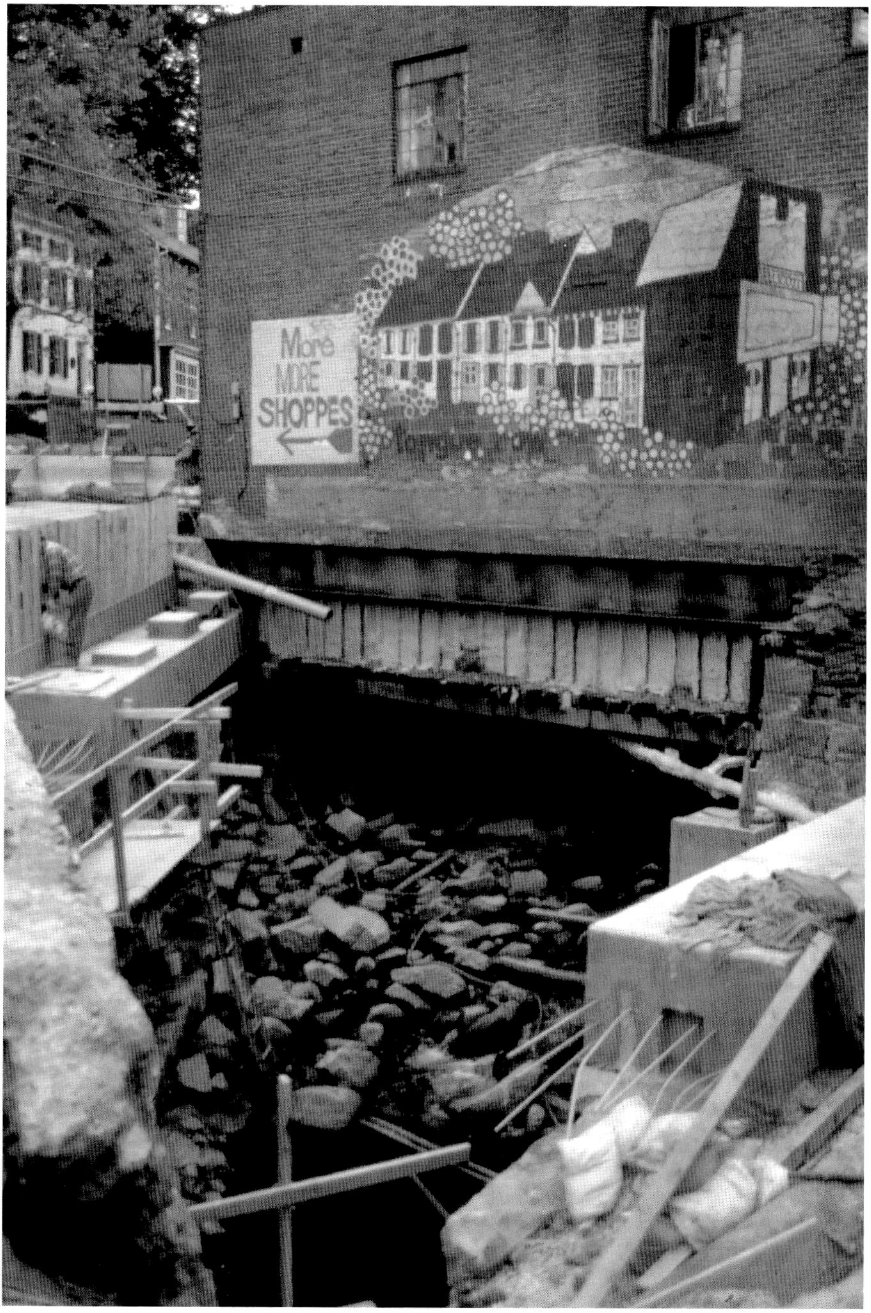

The Tiber Branch of the river, exposed under Columbia Pike. *Courtesy of Herb Johl.*

The Fire of 1999: Memories of Victoria Goeller, Janet Kusterer and Jared Spahn

A carelessly discarded cigarette led to a fire that destroyed six businesses, as well as several apartments on Main Street, in 1999.

"I was home on Court Avenue on the afternoon of Tuesday, November 9, 1999, when I began to hear siren after siren tearing down Main Street," recalled Vickie Goeller, a witness to the event.

> *After fifteen minutes or so I called my husband, George, at his restaurant, the Phoenix Emporium, to ask if something was happening on Main Street. He replied, "It's a fire, a big one." I grabbed my camera and started down Main Street, where groups of people had gathered. I was stopped by police at Fishbein and Fishbein, across the street from the fire, where I was able to take several photographs. Firemen on a ladder truck were dousing flames coming from Main Street Blues and the old Rosenstock building, which housed several businesses. From Caplan's east the street was filled with emergency personnel and equipment.*

Due to the inaccessibility of the street, firefighters were forced to fight the fire by running their hoses through a residence on St. Paul Street that backed up to the site. The restaurant called Main Street Blues was the source of the fire and was destroyed. Three diverse businesses located in the same building were lost—Rugs to Riches, Legend and the Nature Nook.

Locals called the building "the Rosenstock building" after the department store that was located there for many years. Rugs to Riches relocated a few blocks west on Main Street, while Legend, a "New Age, New World" shop, and the Nature Nook, which described itself as making nature accessible to all ages, closed. Next door, Spring House Designs owners found history repeating itself, to their dismay. An arson fire had destroyed a former location, next door to Ellicott's Country Store, on Main Street in 1992. Friends who stored their salvaged inventory reported smelling the unsettling combination of smoke and potpourri. They also closed permanently.

"Determined to reach the Phoenix, I headed up Church Road and began scouting for ways to reach Main Street and stumbled down the hill behind Angelo's Cottage, the white, castle-like landmark on a hill above town," said Goeller.

I emerged just east of Alda Baptiste's Bridal Shop on Main Street and snuck across the street to the Phoenix. Inside, police, firemen and building owners were scrambling for information. Lori Parsons, owner of Cacao Lane Restaurant, the building that housed Side Streets Restaurant and a house on St. Paul's Street, was anxious to reach any of her properties. Her requests were denied. As people were being evacuated from their homes and businesses, they stopped in the Phoenix for information. Unfortunately we had none. As there was nothing for any of us to do except wait and hope for the best, I decided to try to get home. I approached a police officer at Maryland Avenue and St. Paul Street and convinced him to allow me to walk north on the railroad tracks and climb up the hill to Church Road.

Once I arrived home, I sat on my front steps and watched the black smoke rise from lower Main Street. Helicopters began to circle and local television stations began to broadcast nonstop live reports; it felt like Ellicott City was under siege. The Phoenix remained open that night and the phone rang constantly. Main Street was closed from Old Columbia Road to Maryland Avenue. Residents who were unable to reach their homes made their way to the Phoenix hoping for news and comfort.

Early the next morning, George and I set out on foot, hoping to open the Phoenix. Main Street was still closed, packed with police, firemen and their equipment. Luckily we were able to convince the police to let us through. In daylight, we were able to see the utter devastation caused by the fire. Main Street Blues, Rugs to Riches, Legends, the Nature Nook and Spring House Designs—we knew all the owners of these businesses, shopped in their shops and had cocktails at Main Street Blues. All were lost.

As soon as we unlocked the side door of the Phoenix, police and firemen arrived hoping for a cup of coffee. The Phoenix was soon mobbed with tired and hungry emergency personnel. As the morning went on, the Red Cross arrived and set up in our dining room offering assistance to those displaced by the fire. Television reporters camped out in the bar waiting for updates from county officials.

What I remember most are the telephone calls, residents and business owners wondering if their homes and shops were still standing. Calls came from across the country. Ellicott City was truly cut off from the outside world. Soon every available electric outlet in the Phoenix was recharging a resident's cell phone so they could let their friends and families know they were okay. As people were allowed to return to their shops and homes, they would stop in the Phoenix for news about their neighbors. Shelley Harris from Caplan's stopped by for tuna fish. Her cat had been locked in her store and she was hoping the tuna would coax him out from his hiding place.

"I worked as a publicist for both Main Street Blues and Spring House Designs," said Janet Kusterer.

I remember taking my son, Rob, born in 1987, to the Nature Nook as soon as he could walk. They were very kid-friendly—and the kid didn't know he was learning something. Usually a tape would be playing—bird calls, animal growls, other natural sounds. Rob liked to collect the small animal figures they had, each time selecting a different species. They had glow-in-the-dark star decals, perfect to keep a guy company in the dark of his room at night. They had nature T-shirts. Rob found one for his dad for Father's Day one year, covered in fish, front and back. My husband Tom wore it until it fell apart.

When Rob was in middle school, we nurtured his artistic talent with lessons with Bill Sachs at Spring House Design. Bill is an artist who painted a series of Ellicott City historic scenes that grace many local homes today. In each painting, he hides his wife Carole's initials as a special tribute. Carole's end of the business was silk flower arrangements—especially for weddings—and the store was full of them, as well as other gift items. Behind the store, the couple had carved out a small garden next to the stream. As soon after the fire as I could, I visited Spring House. There was no electricity—the only light came from the gaping hole in the back of the building, rubble where the tiny garden once flourished. The smell was damp and dank, the mood so sad. After two fires in two Main Street locations, the Sachses were leaving.

The day of the fire I was scheduled to attend a fundraiser at the Railroad Station Museum for County Councilman Chris Merdon. After the event had to be canceled, volunteers distributed the party food to the firefighters. The day after the fire, I attended a meeting with other historic district residents and businesspeople hosted by County Executive Jim Robey at the Phoenix Emporium. Main Street was still closed to traffic, so to get from my home west of the historic district I had to take a circuitous route, making the usual ten-minute drive take forty minutes. Robey was there to reassure everyone that every effort was being made to make the area secure so that traffic could proceed again. And so the long restoration process began.

"I remember the day of the fire of 1999 very well," said Jared Spahn.

> *I was driving down Rogers Avenue and I saw a tower of smoke at the bottom of Main Street, where my office was at the time. I didn't want to try to drive down there for fear of getting stuck, so I parked at the top of the street and walked down to the front of the Howard House to see what I could see. I called my office, at 8000 Main Street, and asked them to look outside and see what was going on. When they told me about the fire, I decided to go home and get some sleep, as I knew the next day there would be a lot to do. My father called me around 8:00 p.m. and asked me to come back, as we had a lot of planning to do for the next day. The fire was bad. The building where the fire started, Main Street Blues Restaurant, was owned by someone who lived in Ohio. The rest of the buildings involved were owned by Dr. Taylor.*
>
> *The next morning, I met with my dad, Public Works director Jim Irvin and County Executive Jim Robey to assess the damage and see what had to be done to reopen the street. One of the damaged stores had stocked Beanie Babies and we discovered that people had been in the store pilfering them, as well as taking the water-damaged furniture from Rugs to Riches. We learned that the third floor of the Rosenstock building had to be removed before the street could be reopened to cars and pedestrians. I ended up making a lot of calls to find a crane big enough to do the job. The crane removed the third floor and the street reopened within twenty-four hours.*
>
> *I became the central point of contact for the demolition operation. We put up a wooden fence to enclose the construction site. Don Reuwer got students from Glenelg Country Day School to come down and paint murals of Ellicott City scenes on it. We also put windows in the fence so people could watch the progress we were making. We hired architect Greg Mitchell of GMA and D to design the new Rosenstock building. We entered into a six-month-long charette process with the insurance company, who wanted us to rebuild the building as three separate shops, while Dr. Taylor wanted to return it to one building. In the end, we worked it out with the Department of Inspections, Licenses and Permits and were allowed to convert back to one building.*
>
> *Since the building was in the flood plain, we had to deal with FEMA. They don't allow new construction in flood plains so* [they] *wanted us to leave the area as open space. As we knew that most buildings over eighty years old in town had suffered from a fire in the past, we thought that if all of us weren't allowed to rebuild the town would cease to exist. So, we*

were able to get the project officially recognized as a renovation, which can be done in a flood plain. In investigating the fire, it was determined that while the buildings had sprinklers, all the valves were closed. It couldn't be determined how or when that happened.

FEMA wanted us to build a flood-resistant building. Dr. Taylor said, since this was the third building of his that had burned in the historic district, he wanted a building that was completely noncombustible. Meanwhile, we had to deal with the rules of the Historic District Commission, who have to approve of the design. It is hard to build a building compatible with the historic look of the town without using any wood. Dave Hammerman, of the Department of Inspections, Licenses and Permits, said we'd have to build a "modern Noah's Ark."

The way Ellicott City floods is from water backing up from the rivers, so we needed a building that could withstand the hydrostatic pressure of the rising water. The bay windows on the front of the new building hide walls that rise over two feet above the height the water reached during Tropical Storm Agnes, so it would have to flood to that height to get into the building—we also installed special flood doors and placed the electrical services on the second floor to maintain power. It is also fire resistant, made of steel and fiberglass. The window frames are wood, but are clad with aluminum. The building is very secure and could be a safe place for people to go in the event they could not evacuate the area fast enough in case of a flood. The building has a balcony effect on the second floor, similar to nearby historic structures.

"Second-story porches were very common on Main Street in the past," according to Jean Hannon.

Second-story doors are visible today, and early pictures show a series of second-story porches along the lower end of Main Street. It was possible to walk the length of many buildings without ever having to set foot in the mud and debris created by the horses and farm animals on the lower level. It was possible to leave the B&O Station at Ellicott City, enter the Patapsco Hotel porch and proceed along its boardwalk to the Opera House farther up Main Street without ever touching the ground.

"We took the design process to the Historic District Commission," continued Spahn.

We wanted the building to fit in but not to look like it was 150 years old. All the buildings in the historic district were not built at the same time; so many different periods are represented. We worked with the existing color palettes, and added balconies similar to others on Main Street. The design process took a year, with construction taking an additional sixteen months—it was very laborious. When we asked for a staging area for materials and equipment, we got one parking space. We could understand, as the other businesses on the street needed to stay in business, but it was very hard.

This was the most difficult construction project we ever did. The new Rosenstock building has a steel superstructure with a concrete center. Concrete planks were used as prebuilt concrete floors. They extend over the river and are each twenty feet wide and weighed two and a half tons, requiring a huge crane to install them, and footers fifteen feet deep. From the fire to the finished building took two and a half years.

The fire was on November 9. At the time, I was also president of the Ellicott City Business Association, and I was worried that this work would disrupt our town events, especially Midnight Madness just a month later. It was very challenging, but we were able to hold the event.

LOOKING AHEAD

Over 235 years ago, the Ellicott brothers knew a good thing when they saw it and moved to this area to create thriving businesses and thriving families. All these years later, the area is still one of the most desirable in the United States, although it attracts families for far different reasons. In 2008, *Forbes* magazine ranked Howard County—the only Maryland county rated—as number seventeen in its list of best places to raise a family in the United States. The magazine noted its best library system and second highest SAT scores. The same year, *Money* magazine rated Ellicott City and Columbia number eight in its list of best places to live, noting its "mix of charm, comfort and careful zoning." This follows high rankings in other lists published by *Sports Illustrated*, the *American Business Journal* and *CNN Money*. Its enviable location, situated halfway between Washington, D.C., and Baltimore, should ensure its continued popularity, offering its residents the highest quality of life.

The authors share the sentiments written by Celia Holland in *Ellicott City, Maryland—Mill Town USA*. She said, "If when the tour is completed even a handful of people come to know and to love the little town as does the writer, this work will not have been in vain."

Selected References

Bicentennial Celebration Committee. *Ellicott City Bicentennial Journal.* Ellicott City, MD: Bicentennial Celebration Committee, 1972.

Centennial Committee. *Ellicott City Volunteer Firemen's Association, Inc. 100th Anniversary 1888–1988.* Ellicott City, MD: Centennial Committee, 1988.

Cornelison, Alice, Silas E. Craft Sr. and Lillie Price. *Oral History, Schooling and Contempory History of Blacks in Howard County.* Columbia, MD: NAACP, 1986.

Cramm, Joetta. *History Ellicott City, A Walking Tour.* Woodbine, MD: K&D Limited, Inc., 1996.

———. *A Pictorial History Howard County.* Norfolk, VA: The Donning Company, 1987.

Evans, Charles Worthington, Martha Ellicott Tyson and G. Hunter Bartlett. *Fox, Ellicott, Evans; American Family History.* Cockeysville, MD: Fox, Ellicott, Evans Fund, 1976.

Hafner, Allen B., Jr. *Howard County Police Department, 50th Anniversary Commemorative Album.* 2002.

Historic District Commission. *Ellicott City Historic District Design Guidelines.* Howard County, MD: Historic District Commission, 1998.

Historic Ellicott City, Inc. *Heritage Paper.* Ellicott City, MD: Historic Ellicott City, Inc., 1974–1987.

Holland, Celia M., Janet P. Kusterer and Charlotte Holland. *Ellicott City, Maryland—Mill Town, USA*. Ellicott City, MD: Historic Ellicott City, Inc., 2003.

Howard County, MD Sesquicentennial Committee. *Profiles of Faith*. Howard County, MD: Sesquicentennial Committee, 2001.

Hurry, Robert J. *The Discovery and Archeological Investigation of the Benjamin Banneker Homestead Baltimore County*. Crownsville: Maryland Historical Trust Press, 2002.

Kusterer, Janet, and Victoria Goeller. *Then and Now: Ellicott City.* Charleston, SC: Arcadia Publishing, 2006.

Kusterer, Janet, Travis Harry and Charles Kyler. *The Ellicott City B&O Railroad Station Museum*. Ellicott City, MD: Historic Ellicott City, Inc., 2005.

Peirce, James Walker. *A Guide to Patapsco Valley Mill Sites: Our Valley's Contribution to Maryland's Industrial Revolution*. Bloomington, IN: Author House, 2004.

Sharp, Henry K. *The Patapsco River Valley*. Baltimore: Maryland Historical Society, 2001.

Shipley, B.H., Jr. *Remembrances of Passing Days.* Virginia Beach, VA: The Donning Company, 1997.

The Times Newspapers. *The Flood of 1972*. Ellicott City, MD: The Times Newspapers, 1972.

Travers, Paul J. *The Patapsco: Baltimore's River of History.* Centerville, MD: Tidewater Publishers, 1990.

Wolf, Anne, and Dan Wolf. *The Patapsco Guards*. Parts I and II. Howard County, MD: Howard County Genealogical Society, 1997, 2001.